Principles and Standards for School Mathematics Navigations Series

NAVIGATING
through
PROBLEM SOLVING
and
REASONING
in
GRADE 4

Karol L. Yeatts
Michael T. Battista
Sally Mayberry
Denisse R. Thompson
Judith S. Zawojewski

Bonnie H. Litwiller
Grades 3–6 Editor

Peggy A. House
Navigations Series Editor

NCTM®

NATIONAL COUNCIL OF
TEACHERS OF MATHEMATICS

Navigating through problem solving and reasoning in grade 4 / Karol L. Yeatts ...
[et al.] ; grades 3–6 editor, Bonnie H. Litwiller.
    p. cm.
    Includes bibliographical references.
    ISBN 0–87353–574–X
    1. Mathematics—Study and teaching (Elementary) — Activity programs. 2.
Fourth grade (Education)—Activity programs. 3. Problem solving in children
I. Yeatts, Karol L. II. Litwiller, Bonnie H.
    QA135.6 .N37 2005
    372.7′049—dc22

                                                                        200501333

The National Council of Teachers of Mathematics is a public voice of mathematics education, providing vision, leadership, and professional development to support teachers in ensuring mathematics learning of the highest quality for all students.

Printed in the United States of America

Navigations Series

Table of Contents

Contents of the CD-ROM

Introduction

Table of Standards and Expectations, Process Standards, Pre-K–Grade 12

Applet

2-D Shape Decomposition Tool

Blackline Masters and Templates

All blackline titles listed above plus the following:

Box Office Gross Receipts for *Shrek 2*

Web Sites for Interesting Measurement Facts

Sample Student Work for "Movie Money Matters"

Sample Student Work for "Did You Know?"

Sample Student Work for "Analyzing Data for Dr. Angus"

Readings and Supplemental Materials

Strategies for Advancing Children's Mathematical Thinking
Judith Fraivillig
Teaching Children Mathematics

Mathematical Tasks and Student Cognition: Classroom-Based Factors That Support and Inhibit High-Level Mathematical Thinking and Reasoning
Marjorie Henningsen and Mary Kay Stein
Journal for Research in Mathematics Education

Ryan's Primes
Bill Juraschek and Amy Evans
Teaching Children Mathematics

Ideas: Every Beat of Your Heart
Lisa M. Passarello and Francis Fennell
Arithmetic Teacher

Redefining Success in Mathematics Teaching and Learning
Margaret Schwan Smith
Mathematics Teaching in the Middle School

Selecting and Creating Mathematical Tasks: From Research to Practice
Margaret Schwan Smith and Mary Kay Stein
Mathematics Teaching in the Middle School

Mathematical Tasks as a Framework for Reflection: From Research to Practice
Mary Kay Stein and Margaret Schwan Smith
Mathematics Teaching in the Middle School

Making Connections with Prime Numbers
Arlene Yolles
Mathematics Teaching in the Middle School

Polishing a Data Task: Seeking Better Assessment
Judith S. Zawojewski
Teaching Children Mathematics

About This Book

Navigating through Problem Solving and Reasoning in Grade 4 is the fifth of seven grade-level books that present investigations designed to develop students' reasoning methods and problem-solving strategies. The introduction to the book provides an overview of reasoning and problem solving as they might appear in grade 4. A discussion of the role of the teacher in nurturing the development of students' reasoning and problem-solving abilities comes next. Five explorations follow, each situated in a different one of the five content strands identified in *Principles and Standards for School Mathematics* (National Council of Teachers of Mathematics [NCTM] 2000)—number and operations, algebra, geometry, measurement, and data analysis and probability. For the convenience of the teacher, the Standards and expectations for the Process Standards (which include Problem Solving as well as Reasoning and Proof) appear on the inside front cover of the book.

All the explorations are organized in the same way:

- Focus
- Overview
- Goals
- Mathematical Content
- Prior Knowledge or Experience
- Materials
- Classroom Environment
- Investigation
- Assessment
- Reflections
- Connections

Three different icons appear in this book, as shown in the key. One alerts readers to material quoted from *Principles and Standards for School Mathematics*, another points them to supplementary materials on the CD-ROM that accompanies the book, and a third signals the blackline masters and indicates their locations in the appendix.

All the investigations have blackline masters, which are signaled in the text by an icon. These activity pages are identified in the materials list for the explorations and appear—along with the solutions to the problems—in the appendix. You can also print the blackline pages from the CD-ROM that accompanies the book. The CD, also signaled by an icon, contains an applet for your students to manipulate and resources for your professional development.

Margin notes present suggestions to aid you in preparing to use the investigations in your classroom. As your students work, take note of the appropriateness of their mathematics vocabularies, the clarity of their explanations, and the complexity of their solutions. Such observations will be helpful in designing adaptations of the activities for students with special educational needs.

Key to Icons

Principles and Standards

CD-ROM

Blackline Master

Although this book emphasizes reasoning and problem solving, it is not intended to be a complete curriculum for developing reasoning methods and problem-solving strategies in fourth grade. We encourage you instead to use it in conjunction with other instructional materials.

The authors gratefully acknowledge the contributions of Caroline F. Borrow and Judy Melillo for their work with Michael T. Battista on Making and Investigating Puzzles and of Margret Hjalmarson for her collaboration with Judith S. Zawojewski on Growing Giant Sequoias. Special thanks go to the teachers and students at Mount Vernon Elementary School, St. Petersburg, Florida, who worked with Denisse Thompson to pilot Fascinating Measures and to Tammy Keiper and her students at Campbell Park Elementary School, St. Petersburg, Florida, for their insights into the final version of the investigation.

NAVIGATIONS SERIES

GRADE 4

PROBLEM SOLVING *and* REASONING

Introduction

Principles and Standards for School Mathematics (NCTM 2000) states that "problem solving is the cornerstone of school mathematics. Without the ability to solve problems, the usefulness and power of mathematical ideas, knowledge, and skills are severely limited" (p. 182). Mathematical investigations that challenge students to deal with nonroutine problems and situations should be a regular part of Standards-based instruction at all levels.

Just as solving problems can help students make sense of their changing world, justifying solutions and communicating the results of mathematical investigations can help elementary school students develop and expand their reasoning abilities. One goal is for students to develop ways of thinking about mathematics that encourage sense making and reasoning about solutions and strategies. The mathematics classroom is the main environment in which students speak and write mathematics. Hence, it is essential that teachers offer students opportunities to communicate mathematically by having them make, test, discuss, and refine conjectures, ultimately accepting or rejecting them.

The investigations in this book engage students in extended tasks that enable them to look for relationships among concepts in the five content strands—number and operations, algebra, geometry, measurement, and data analysis and probability. Each investigation enables students to focus on one strand in depth. At the same time, the investigations illustrate how a carefully chosen mathematical task can bridge content areas. For example, although the focus of the data analysis investigation is on analyzing data and drawing conclusions from them, students work with numerical computations involving averaging, working with decimal numbers, and making metric measurements.

Aspects of Problem Solving

Good problems challenge students to develop and apply strategies, serve as a means to introduce new concepts, and offer a context for using skills. Problem solving is not a specific topic to be taught but a process that permeates all mathematics.

What behaviors might a teacher expect to observe in a classroom that makes problem solving a focus? According to *Principles and Standards for School Mathematics*, all students should—

- build new mathematical knowledge through problem solving;
- solve problems that arise in mathematics and in other contexts;
- apply and adapt a variety of appropriate strategies to solve problems; and
- monitor and reflect on the process of mathematical problem solving. (NCTM 2000, p. 402)

Fourth-grade students have an opportunity to engage in problem solving as they complete the investigations in this book, discuss their ideas and conjectures in pairs or small groups, and justify their thinking to the teacher and other members of the class. As teachers facilitate the investigations, the tasks naturally lead to such questions as "Why?" and "How do you know?"

Students build new mathematical knowledge through problem solving

Students can learn new mathematical concepts and skills through problem solving. A successful problem-centered approach uses interesting problems to motivate students to spend time and energy and be persistent in seeking solutions. Under the guidance of a teacher who encourages students to reason creatively and make connections between ideas, students can discover new mathematical concepts, techniques, and relationships. New ideas often emerge from discussions among students. Teachers should guide such discussions carefully so that the students learn the difference between correct mathematical reasoning and incorrect reasoning and between sound problem-solving strategies and unsound ones. The teacher must summarize classroom discussions so that the students are aware of the new knowledge and skills that they have derived from the problem-solving experience.

Students solve problems that arise in mathematics and other contexts

The investigations in this book pose problems to solve in contexts that are mathematically rich, appeal to fourth graders, and facilitate communication skills. In Discovering Primes As the Ancient Mathematicians Did, students begin with a scenario in which some other students are trying to solve a challenging problem to get their teacher to participate in a dunking booth at a carnival. In Movie Money Matters, students explore contracts between theater owners and movie distributors and, in the process, calculate mathematical change over

"Students who can both develop and carry out a plan to solve a mathematical problem are exhibiting knowledge that is much deeper and more useful than simply carrying out a computation." (NCTM 2000, p. 182)

time. Making and Investigating Puzzles gives students experience in decomposing and recomposing two-dimensional puzzles. In Fascinating Measures, students find their heart rate for a minute and use the results to determine their number of heartbeats in a year and predict their number of heartbeats in a lifetime. In Growing Giant Sequoias, students interpret a set of data to determine the lighting conditions that appear to improve the growth of tree seedlings. In each of these investigations, students grapple with problems that arise in real-world situations. The problems are interesting and challenging vehicles for exploring mathematics and thinking about relationships.

Students apply and adapt a variety of strategies to solve problems

As students explore problems, they need to consider a variety of strategies to investigate the solution. In Movie Money Matters, students represent profits by plotting points and creating bar graphs and tables. In Growing Giant Sequoias, different groups of students use different approaches to extrapolate data for missing tree heights and represent their approaches through graphs or tables. The varied representations afford students many different ways to explore a problem and enable those with different learning styles to benefit from the problem-solving experience.

Students monitor and reflect on the process of mathematical problem solving

As students work through good mathematical tasks, they reflect on their work to determine what strategies are effective and where they need to make adjustments. In Making and Investigating Puzzles, students investigate cutting two-dimensional figures to produce specific new shapes, and they investigate puzzle pieces to determine which ones have specific characteristics (e.g., line symmetry or rotation symmetry). Students are encouraged to make a conjecture and then test it. By monitoring what happens when they try to fit a piece in the puzzle, students become much more proficient in making conjectures. In Fascinating Measures, students use a multistep problem-solving process to determine the number of heartbeats in an hour, a day, or a year. They then apply this same process to other measurement facts to represent the measure in an equivalent way that is easier to understand. By reflecting on the process that they use with one problem, students can build a repertoire of problem-solving strategies that they can apply to a wide range of problems.

Aspects of Reasoning

Reasoning develops over time as teachers facilitate discussion of rich tasks and help students learn "to construct valid arguments and to evaluate the arguments of others" (NCTM 2000, p. 188). As students reason about mathematics, they should—

"Reflecting on different ways of thinking about and representing a problem solution allows comparisons of strategies and consideration of different representations." (NCTM 2000, p. 185)

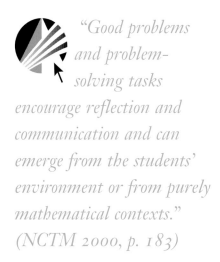

"Good problems and problem-solving tasks encourage reflection and communication and can emerge from the students' environment or from purely mathematical contexts." (NCTM 2000, p. 183)

- make and investigate mathematical conjectures;
- develop and evaluate mathematical arguments and proofs; and
- select and use various types of reasoning and methods of proof. (NCTM 2000, p. 402)

Students make and investigate mathematical conjectures

Students need to learn that making conjectures on the basis of patterns is a natural part of mathematical thinking. In Discovering Primes As the Ancient Mathematicians Did, students use the Sieve of Eratosthenes to find how many prime numbers exist between 1 and 100. In Making and Investigating Puzzles, students think about the properties of puzzle pieces and make a conjecture about whether a piece will fit before actually trying it.

Students develop and evaluate mathematical arguments and proofs

In Movie Money Matters, students compare different contracts between theater owners and movie distributors and discuss which contracts should be renegotiated. In Growing Giant Sequoias, students consider growing tree seedlings in sun or shade, develop a process to determine which lighting condition is better, present their process to the class, and then adjust it on the basis of feedback from other students.

Students select and use various types of reasoning and methods of justification

Throughout the investigations, students have opportunities to justify their reasoning in several ways. The algebra investigation, Movie Money Matters, prompts students to evaluate different contracts to determine which one provides the largest profits for the theater owners and the movie distributors. In the geometry investigation, Making and Investigating Puzzles, students reason by making conjectures and then testing those conjectures on the computer or by physically making puzzle pieces. The data analysis investigation, Growing Giant Sequoias, encourages students to reason by applying a proposed plan to evaluate which lighting condition is better for the growth of tree seedlings.

The Role of the Teacher

As students explore the tasks in this book, their teachers should monitor their activities and foster the interactions necessary to maintain high levels of reasoning. (See Stein and Smith [1998]). The tasks are mathematically rich, but if teachers provide too many clues or too much specific help early in the process, they can stifle the deep thinking that the tasks can elicit from students. The challenge for teachers is to facilitate students' communication about a task without directing the students toward a particular solution.

From detailed observations in an elementary school classroom using a Standards-based curriculum, Fraivillig (2001) has identified various strategies that are essential to helping students think deeply about mathematical ideas and share their thinking with others. These approaches fall into three broad categories: eliciting students' thinking, supporting students' thinking, and extending students' thinking. Descriptions of the strategies in each category are summarized in figure 1.

Fig. **1.**

Strategies to advance students' thinking

Strategies to elicit students' thinking

- Elicit many solution methods for one problem.
- Wait for, and listen to, students' descriptions of solution methods.
- Encourage students to elaborate and discuss.
- Use students' explanations as a basis for the lesson's content.
- Convey an attitude of acceptance of students' errors and efforts.
- Promote collaborative problem solving.

Strategies to support students' thinking

- Remind students of conceptually similar problems.
- Provide background knowledge.
- Lead students through "instant replays." (Revisit student solutions.)
- Write symbolic representations of solutions when appropriate.

Strategies to extend students' thinking

- Maintain high standards and expectations for all students.
- Encourage students to make generalizations.
- List all solution methods on the board to promote reflection.
- Push individual students to try alternative solution methods.
- Promote the use of more efficient solution methods.

Adapted from Fraivillig (2001, pp. 454–59)

In addition, research from the Quantitative Understanding Amplifying Student Achievement and Reasoning (QUASAR) Project in urban schools with underachieving students found that the following actions by teachers were associated with higher performance by their students on a test of problem solving (Henningsen and Stein 1997; Stein, Grover, and Henningsen 1996; Smith and Stein 1998):

- Teachers press for explanations and meaning.
- Teachers have capable students model high-level performance.
- Teachers allow appropriate time for students to explore the task, think, and make sense of mathematics for themselves.
- Teachers note conceptual connections.
- Teachers build on students' prior knowledge.

See Fraivillig (2001) on the CD-ROM for classroom strategies that elicit, support, and extend students' thinking.

See Henningsen and Stein (1997), Smith and Stein (1998), and Stein and Smith (1998) on the CD-ROM for ideas on using mathematical tasks to stimulate reflection.

Teachers who engage in behaviors like those identified by Fraivillig and the QUASAR researchers can help students develop their reasoning and problem-solving abilities. Teachers can use the following questions to help elicit students' reasoning:

- "Why?"
- "How do you know?"
- "What other problems can you remember that are similar to this one?"
- "Are there other ways you could solve this problem?"
- "Do you agree with this approach to this problem? Why, or why not?"

Such questions can stimulate important teacher-student discourse that will strengthen the reasoning abilities of all students and can engage students in mathematical communication in the classroom.

The role of the teacher is indispensable, and the investigations in this book are designed to help teachers encourage problem solving and reasoning by elementary school mathematics students. Engaging students in these processes is an essential component of developing their mathematical power.

NAVIGATIONS SERIES

GRADE 4

PROBLEM
SOLVING
and REASONING

Investigations

Discovering Primes As the Ancient Mathematicians Did

Focus

Reasoning about number relationships

Overview

Students in grade 4 should "understand numbers, ways of representing numbers, relationships among numbers, and number systems" and be able to "describe classes of numbers according to characteristics such as their factors" (NCTM 2000, p. 148). In this investigation, fourth graders explore the concepts of *factor* and *prime*. Using divisibility rules, a hundreds chart, and the Sieve of Eratosthenes, they can begin to relate these mathematical concepts to real life.

Goals

- Define, differentiate among, and apply factors, multiples, prime numbers, and composite numbers in mathematical situations
- Use the Sieve of Eratosthenes to identify prime numbers

Mathematical Content

This investigation supports the following Number and Operations and Process Standards and expectations for grades 3–5 (NCTM 2000, pp. 392, 402):

Number and Operations

- Understand numbers, ways of representing numbers, relationships among numbers, and number systems

Problem Solving

- Build new mathematical knowledge through problem solving
- Monitor and reflect on the process of mathematical problem solving

Reasoning and Proof

- Make and investigate mathematical conjectures

Students in fourth grade learn to represent numbers by their factors. Learning to distinguish prime numbers from composite numbers is important for the understanding of numbers, particularly with respect to multiplication and division of whole numbers and renaming fractions.

For students to develop their thinking skills, they must believe that they are working in a safe classroom environment where risk taking is acceptable and errors are learning opportunities. When teachers support and extend students' mathematical understanding, students can safely reach out and try new mathematical ideas. In applying the concepts of prime numbers and factors, students need to develop a clear understanding of the meaning of these mathematical ideas.

Students in grade 4 should "understand numbers, ways of representing numbers, relationships among numbers, and number systems" and be able to "describe classes of numbers according to characteristics such as their factors." (NCTM 2000, p. 148).

"Instructional programs ... should enable all students to understand numbers, ways of representing numbers, relationships among numbers, and number systems." (NCTM 2000, p. 392)

Prior Knowledge or Experience

• A beginning understanding of place value, factors, multiples, and divisors

Materials

For each student—

• A copy of each of the following blackline masters:
  ○ "Using the Sieve of Eratosthenes"
  ○ "Hundreds Chart"
• Six crayons or markers in different colors (the investigation uses green, red, blue, yellow, orange, and purple)

Classroom Environment

Students work in pairs, using the Sieve of Eratosthenes to identify prime numbers on a hundreds chart.

Investigation

Present the following scenario to your students:

Oceanside Elementary School is preparing for its annual spring carnival. Mr. Johnson has issued a challenge to his fourth-grade students. If his class can determine the total number of prime numbers on a hundreds chart, he will volunteer to participate in the "Dunk the Teacher" booth at the carnival. Mr. Johnson suggests that students use the procedure for the Sieve of Eratosthenes as they try to meet his challenge.

After you have read the scenario, provide the following background information:

In ancient Greece a man named Eratosthenes developed a method for finding prime numbers. Eratosthenes was an outstanding scholar who lived between 275 and 195 B.C. He was born in Cyrene, on the northern coast of Africa, grew up in Athens, and later moved to Alexandria, in Egypt. Eratosthenes was known as a mathematician, an astronomer, a geographer, a poet, and a librarian (he served as director of the Library in Alexandria). He was responsible for many varied discoveries in the ancient world—for example, he was the first person to arrive at an accurate estimate for the earth's diameter. Eratosthenes also created a method of identifying prime numbers that we now call the Sieve of Eratosthenes. A sieve is a strainer. An everyday example of a sieve is a colander, a kitchen utensil that holds cooked spaghetti while the water drains through many holes.

Read aloud to the class the story *The Librarian Who Measured the Earth* by Kathryn Lasky. Mixing history and science, Lasky tells how Eratosthenes calculated the circumference of the earth through a process involving the sun and shadows.

Group your students in pairs and distribute copies of the blackline masters "Using the Sieve of Eratosthenes" and "Hundreds Chart" to

pp. 52–53; 54

A *prime number* is a whole number with exactly two distinct factors, itself and 1. (For example, 3 is a prime number because its only factors are 3 and 1.)

A *composite number* is a whole number that has more than two factors. (For instance, 4 is a composite number because it has three factors: 1, 2, and 4.)

A *factor* is a whole number component of a multiplication computation. (The number 15 has the factors 1, 3, 5, and 15, for example.)

A *multiple* is a whole number product of a given number. (The multiples of 3 are 3, 6, 9, 12, and so on.)

Note: The number 1 is neither a prime nor a composite number because it does not have two distinct factors.

each student. Ask, "Do you think the fourth graders at Oceanside Elementary School will be able to rise to Mr. Johnson's challenge and find all the prime numbers on a hundreds chart?" Your students will probably see the goal of dunking Mr. Johnson at the carnival as well worth the Oceanside students' efforts to find the primes. Say, "See if you and your partner can use the procedure of the Sieve of Eratosthenes and find the answer to Mr. Johnson's question."

If you wish, you can offer your students an incentive, though probably not an opportunity to dunk you! You might give them extra time for independent reading, extended time on the playground, or a night without mathematics homework, for example.

Procedure for Using the Sieve of Eratosthenes

Begin by asking the students, "How many prime numbers do you think exist between 1 and 100?" Have the students cross off the number 1 on the hundreds chart because it is not prime. Remind them that a prime number has exactly two factors—itself and 1—and the factors must be different from each other.

Have the students circle the number 2 in green. It has exactly two factors—itself and 1—so it is prime. They can use green to cross off all the multiples of 2 on their chart. Each of these numbers has at least three factors—1, 2, and the number itself—so none of them is a prime. Have the students examine the pattern that the crossed-off numbers make on the chart. Ask them, "Does the pattern help you discover anything about the numbers that are multiples of 2? Can you come up with a rule about the numbers that you can divide evenly by 2?"

Now have the students circle the number 3 in red. It has exactly two factors—itself and 1—so it is prime. Use red to cross off all the multiples of 3. Each of these numbers has at least three factors—1, 3, and the number itself—so none of them is a prime. The students may discover that they have already crossed off some of the multiples of 3 in green. If so, they should cross them off again in red.

As the students examine the pattern of crossed-off numbers on the chart now, ask them if the pattern helps them discover anything about the numbers that are multiples of 3. You could say, "Here's a hint: Consider the number 6. You have crossed it off in both red and green. This means that 6 has both 2 and 3 as factors, so 6 is a multiple of both 2 and 3." Ask the students to come up with a rule about numbers that they can divide evenly by 3.

The students have already crossed off the number 4 on their charts, so move to the number 5. Have them use blue to circle the 5—another prime because it also has exactly two factors (itself and 1)—and cross off all the multiples of 5. Each of these numbers has at least three factors. If the students have already crossed off any of these numbers in green or red, have them cross it off again in blue. Say, "Look at the pattern of crossed-off numbers on your chart now. Does the pattern help you discover anything about the numbers that are multiples of 5? Can you come up with a rule about numbers that you can divide evenly by 5?"

Have the students repeat the process that they have been following for circling prime numbers and crossing off numbers that are multiples. They should use a different color each time and continue working until the chart has no numbers left to cross off or circle. They should write

Navigating through Problem Solving and Reasoning in Grade 4

down any discoveries that the color patterns help them make and list any rules that they come up with about numbers that they can divide evenly by a particular prime number. Ask them, "How many prime numbers have you managed to 'catch' in your sieve? Name them."

Divisibility "Rules"

The investigation prompts the students to consider the patterns in the numbers that they cross off from their hundreds charts. In examining these patterns, your students may discover for themselves some of the characteristics of numbers that are evenly divisible by particular divisors. Figure 2 shows divisibility "rules" for divisors from 2 to 10.

Fig. **2.**

Divisibility "rules"

Divisor	Characteristics of a number that is evenly divisible by the divisor
2	The number is even. (That is, the units digit is 0, 2, 4, 6, or 8.)
3	The sum of the digits is divisible by 3.
4	The last two digits form a number that is divisible by 4.
5	The units digit is 5 or zero.
6	The number is divisible by both 2 and 3.
7	If you can double the units digit, subtract the product from the remaining digits, and obtain a new number that is divisible by 7, then the original number is also divisible by 7.
8	The last three digits form a number that is divisible by 8. (No example appears on a hundreds chart because there are only one-, two-, and three-digit numbers.)
9	The sum of all the digits is divisible by 9.
10	The units digit is zero.

Suppose that you have the number 161, and you want to know if it is divisible by 7.

- Take the units digit: 1.
- Double it: $1 \times 2 = 2$.
- Subtract your product from the remaining digits: $16 - 2 = 14$.
- Determine if the difference is divisible by 7: $14 \div 7 = 2$.
- If it is, then your original number is also divisible by 7: $161 \div 7 = 23$.

Suppose that you have the number 2432, and you want to know if it is divisible by 8.

- Take the last three digits: 432.
- See if they form a number that is divisible by 8: $432 \div 8 = 54$.
- If they do, then the original is divisible by 8: $2432 \div 8 = 304$.

Do not expect your students to discover all the rules. For example, the rules for divisibility by 7 and 8 are complex, and students have no real opportunity to discover them in their work with the numbers on a hundreds chart. The rule for divisibility by 7 is most useful for numbers of three or more digits, and the rule for divisibility by 8 applies only to numbers of more than three digits. Nevertheless, you may wish to demonstrate these rules to your students (the margin shows applications of them).

After the students have completed their search for prime numbers, discuss the following questions:

1. "How many prime numbers did you find in the hundreds chart?" (25)

The prime numbers between 1 and 100 are 2, 3, 5, 7, 11, 13, 17, 19, 23, 29, 31, 37, 41, 43, 47, 53, 59, 61, 67, 71, 73, 79, 83, 89, and 97.

If your students search for primes greater than 100, you may want to allow them to use calculators to find large multiples.

2. "If you wanted to search for the primes in the numbers from 101 to 200, then from 201 to 300, and so forth, how could you do it?" (Extend the Sieve of Eratosthenes to larger charts of numbers, but don't forget to cross out all the multiples of the first 25 primes less than 100.)

3. "What is the first multiple of 7 that you found that you hadn't already crossed off as a multiple of a smaller prime?" (49)

4. "If you had just circled 11 as a prime and were crossing off multiples of 11, what number would you need to have in your chart to be able to cross off a multiple of 11 for the first time?" (121)

5. "How many primes did you find in the first 50 numbers?" (15) "This represents what fraction of all the primes on the hundreds chart?" (3/5)

6. "What is the difference between a prime number and a composite number?" (See the note in the margin on page 9.)

7. "Is the number 1 a prime number? Is it a composite number?" (No, the number 1 is neither prime nor composite.)

8. "What do you think the next five prime numbers after 100 would be?" (101, 103, 107, 109, 113)

Tell your students that the fourth graders at Oceanside Elementary School met the deadline and located all the prime numbers on the hundreds chart. Mr. Johnson did indeed participate in the spring carnival and was frequently dunked at the "Dunk the Teacher" booth.

If you want to extend your students' work with primes, you might tell them that Mr. Johnson later invited his students to explore Goldbach's conjecture, which states that every even number greater than 2 can be expressed as the sum of two primes. Mr. Johnson said he would make up a list of twelve even numbers. If the students can write each of his numbers as a sum of two primes, he will again volunteer on the second day of the spring carnival—this time to be the target in the pie-throwing contest! Ask your students to investigate the conjecture.

In 1742, Christian Goldbach (1690–1764) made the assertion that every even number greater than 2 can be expressed as the sum of two primes. This assertion is called a conjecture because to this day it has never been proved or disproved.

Assessment

Much of the assessment of this activity will be informal, as you observe students participating in the discovery of prime and composite numbers. You might give the students a set of numbers and ask them to identify the primes. Have them give a written explanation of how they determined which numbers were prime.

Reflections

This investigation helps students make the distinction between prime numbers and composite numbers. Fourth-grade students find working with the Sieve of Eratosthenes stimulating and thought provoking.

Various misconceptions hinder students' understanding of prime and composite numbers. For example, students may still confuse the definitions of prime and composite numbers. Allow them to explore with blocks, chips, or paper squares. A prime number of blocks will form a rectangle in only one way (one by the number of blocks), but a composite number of blocks will form a rectangle in more than one way (for example, 12 blocks will form a rectangle that is 1 × 12, 2 × 6, or 3 × 4 blocks).

Connections

This investigation of prime numbers promotes understanding and allows students to use mathematical language, discuss the historical roots of mathematics, and increase their desire for knowledge in other areas of mathematics. Prime numbers are important building blocks because every integer can be written as a product of its prime factors in only one way. This activity will lead to an understanding of prime factorization, factor trees, least common multiples, and greatest common factors and will assist students in their quest to rename fractions.

See Juraschek and Evans (1997) and Yolles (2001) on the CD-ROM for additional ideas on teaching about primes.

Movie Money Matters

Focus

Reasoning about algebraic relationships

Overview

Students in fourth grade are continuing to develop an understanding of the idea that they can use algebra to model geometric and numerical patterns. Students should have experiences in creating graphs from tables of values and describing changes in both the values and the graphs. They should use models to predict and draw conclusions about the situations being modeled.

Change over time is an important mathematical idea. This investigation affords students an opportunity to represent information over time as they create tables, plot points, and construct bar graphs. Students will see how profits of theater owners increase or decrease over time. Further, students will help the theater owners decide whether they should continue their contracts or renegotiate for better ones that will yield higher profits over time.

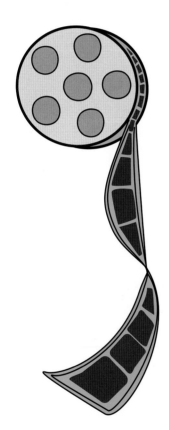

Goals

- Represent and analyze data
- Create models, tables, and graphs to represent the data
- Display different patterns of change, including change that occurs at a constant rate and change that increases or decreases over time

Mathematical Content

This investigation promotes the following Algebra and Process Standards and expectations for grades 3–5 (NCTM 2000, pp. 394, 402).

Algebra

- Understand patterns, relations, and functions
  - Describe, extend, and make generalizations about geometric and numeric patterns
- Use mathematical models to represent and understand quantitative relationships
  - Use representations such as graphs [and] tables to … draw conclusions
- Analyze change in various contexts
  - Identify and describe situations with constant or varying rates of change and compare them

Problem Solving

- Apply and adapt a variety of appropriate strategies to solve problems

Communication

- Organize and consolidate … mathematical thinking through communication

Representation

- Create and use representations to organize, record, and communicate mathematical ideas
- Select, apply, and translate among mathematical representations to solve problems
- Use representations to model and interpret physical, social, and mathematical phenomena

Students in grades 3–5 should have opportunities to investigate situations pertaining to different patterns of change, including change that occurs at a constant rate and change whose rate increases or decreases over time. Fourth-grade students should be encouraged to use models of representation, such as tables and graphs, as they learn to analyze change in various contexts. Providing opportunities for students to construct and interpret a variety of representations will help them become skilled in selecting effective ways to represent problem situations.

In fourth grade, algebra should emphasize models for representing and finding patterns. The focus in elementary grades is on thinking and reasoning, both of which are fundamental to developing an understanding of algebra.

Students in fourth grade need support and guidance as they begin using tables and graphs to analyze change in various contexts.

Prior Knowledge or Experience

- Examining patterns
- Setting up data tables
- Plotting points and constructing bar graphs
- Computing with fractions

Materials

For each group of students—

- A copy of each of the following blackline masters:

  ○ "Movie Money Matters"
  ○ "Movie Distributor's Profit" (optional)
  ○ "Theater Owner's Profit" (optional)

- Access to spreadsheet software (optional)

For each student—

- Centimeter grid paper (available as a blackline master)
- A calculator

pp. 55, 56, 57, 58

Classroom Environment

After the opening scenario is presented to the whole class, the students work in groups of four to six members. Each group chooses to be the consultant team for one of the three theater owners or the consultant team for one of the three movie distributors. At the end of the investigation, the students present their data to the entire class, and the class decides which contract will yield the greatest profit for both the theater owners and the movie distributors.

Investigation

Present the following scenario to the students:

Three theater owners are showing the same hit movie. The movie has been playing for the past five weeks and will play at each of the theaters for five more weeks. The box office receipts at each of the three theaters have totaled exactly the same amount, even though each theater owner's contract with the movie distributor is different, and those receipts have steadily increased by a fixed amount each week. Because the movie is a great moneymaker, the theater owners have considered renegotiating their contracts with the movie distributors for the remaining five weeks. Each theater owner wants to earn the greatest profit. Which is the best contract to negotiate? Which contract will yield the greatest profit for the theater owners? Which contract will yield the greatest profit for the movie distributors? Can a contract be written that will yield an equal profit for both the theater owners and the movie distributors? Each theater owner and each movie distributor requires the assistance of a mathematics consulting team to help figure out which is the best contract to sign.

Divide the class into groups of four to six members. Have the groups choose to be the consulting team for one of the theater owners—theater owner 1, 2, or 3—or the consulting team for one of the movie distributors—movie distributor 1, 2, or 3.

Give the students a copy of the blackline master "Movie Money Matters" and centimeter grid paper and a calculator. "Movie Money Matters" includes the contracts for each of the theater owners as well as the box office receipts for the past five weeks for the theaters. The blackline masters "Theater Owner's Profit" and "Movie Distributor's Profit" are optional. The students may use them or construct their own tables. Read aloud each of the theater owner's contracts, as shown in figure 3.

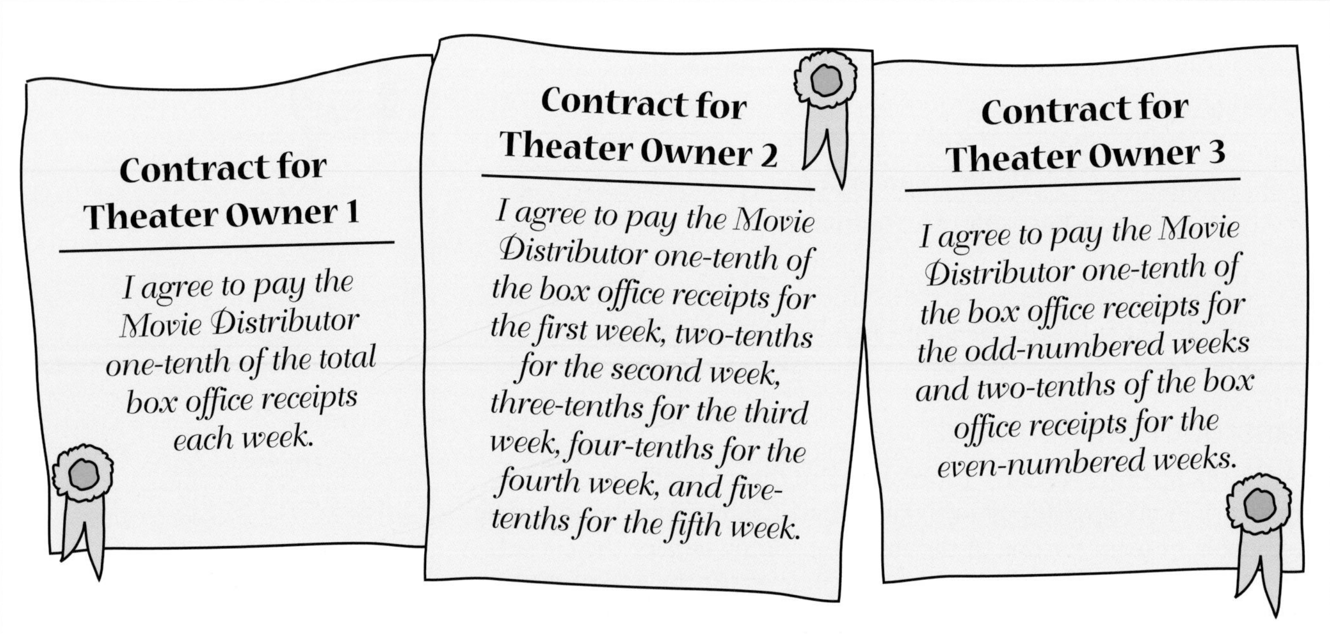

Contract for Theater Owner 1

I agree to pay the Movie Distributor one-tenth of the total box office receipts each week.

Contract for Theater Owner 2

I agree to pay the Movie Distributor one-tenth of the box office receipts for the first week, two-tenths for the second week, three-tenths for the third week, four-tenths for the fourth week, and five-tenths for the fifth week.

Contract for Theater Owner 3

I agree to pay the Movie Distributor one-tenth of the box office receipts for the odd-numbered weeks and two-tenths of the box office receipts for the even-numbered weeks.

Fig. **3**.

Contracts between theater owners and movie distributors

Discuss with the students what is meant by *profit*. Explain that the theater owner does not keep all the money from the sale of the movie tickets. There are many expenses involved in operating a theater, such as the costs of renting the space, paying all the people who work at the theater, and paying for the water and electrical utilities. Most important, the theater owner needs to pay the movie distributor a predetermined amount of money for showing the movie. This amount is part of the contract between the theater owner and the movie distributor. The payment to the movie distributor comes directly from the weekly box office receipts. This investigation refers to this payment as the movie distributor's profit. It refers to the money that the theater owner has left after subtracting the movie distributor's profit from the box office receipts as the theater owner's profit. The theater owner's operating expenses will not be part of this investigation. You may choose to extend this investigation by providing students with an amount for the theater owner's weekly operating expenses and having students then compute the theater owner's net profit.

Give each consulting team a copy of the blackline master "Movie Money Matters," which shows the three theater owners' contracts and the box office receipts for all the theaters for the past five weeks (see also fig. 4).

Box Office Receipts	
Week 1	$1000
Week 2	$2000
Week 3	$3000
Week 4	$4000
Week 5	$5000

Fig. **4**.

Box office receipts for all theaters

Have the students create a table to display each week's box office receipts and each week's profit for both the movie distributor and the theater owner. The students may use the optional blackline masters "Movie Distributor's Profit" and "Theater Owner's Profit" at this time. Explain to the students that to obtain the amount of money that the theater owner will receive weekly they will need to compute the difference between the box office receipts and the amount paid to the movie distributor according to the terms of the contract. Tell the students that they are to compute the profit for the remaining five weeks on the basis of the pattern that they observe in the weekly profits. They will use the pattern to determine how much money the movie distributors and theater owners will earn.

Help your students determine the theater owner's profit

The students working as the consulting team for theater owner 1 should construct a table that shows for each week the box office receipts, the movie distributor's profit, and the theater owner's profit.

For example, theater owner 1 has a contract to pay the movie distributor one-tenth of the total box office receipts each week. The box office receipts for theater 1 for the first five weeks are as follows: week 1—$1000;

week 2—$2000; week 3—$3000; week 4—$4000; and week 5—$5000. The students working as the consulting team for theater owner 1 construct a table that shows, for each week, the box office receipts, how much the theater owner needs to pay the movie distributor, and the amount of the theater owner's profit. After determining the pattern in the weekly increase in the box office receipts and the theater owner's weekly profit, the students then compute the theater owner's profit for the remaining five weeks. A sample chart appears in table 1.

Table 1.
Theater Owner 1's Projected Profit

Week	Box Office Receipts	Amount Paid to Movie Distributor (Box office receipts multiplied by 1/10)	Theater Owner's Profit (Box office receipts minus amount paid to movie distributor)
1	$1000	$1000 × 1/10 = $100	$1000 – $100 = $ 900
2	$2000	$2000 × 1/10 = $200	$2000 – $200 = $1800
3	$3000	$3000 × 1/10 = $300	$3000 – $300 = $2700
4	$4000	$4000 × 1/10 = $400	$4000 – $400 = $3600
5	$5000	$5000 × 1/10 = $500	$5000 – $500 = $4500
6			
7			
8			
9			
10			

Help your students determine the movie distributor's profit

The students working as the consulting team for movie distributor 1, the distributor for theater 1, construct a table that shows for each week the box office receipts and the movie distributor's profit. After determining the pattern in the weekly increase in the box office receipts and the weekly movie distributor's profit, the students then compute the movie distributor's profit for the remaining five weeks. A sample chart appears in table 2.

Help your students create bar graphs to represent profits

After all the student consulting teams have completed their data tables, have them create bar graphs and plot the points on grid paper to represent the profit (see fig. 5). Bar graphs may be displayed either horizontally or vertically. Remind the students to label the bar graphs. When plotting the points, they should also label the *x*- and *y*-axes of the graph. For example, the *x*-axis represents the number of weeks, and the *y*-axis represents the profit. Explain that the intervals on the *x*-axis must be equal and that the intervals on the *y*-axis must also be equal. Remind your students to give their graphs an appropriate title. One example of a table and graph created by students is shown here (see fig. 5). Other work by students appears on the CD-ROM.

For more on graphing, refer to Navigating through Data Analysis and Probability in Grades 3–5 *(Chapin et al. 2002).*

To incorporate technology into the investigation, you can have your students use an electronic spreadsheet program to create their tables and graphs. Several software programs designed for elementary grade levels allow students to create a variety of tables and graphs.

Help your students analyze the rate of change

After your students have constructed their tables and graphs, have them discuss the relationships that they observed among the number of

Table 2.
Movie Distributor 1's Projected Profit

Week	Box Office Receipts	Movie Distributor's Profit (Box office receipts multiplied by 1/10)
1	$1000	$1000 × 1/10 = $100
2	$2000	$2000 × 1/10 = $200
3	$3000	$3000 × 1/10 = $300
4	$4000	$4000 × 1/10 = $400
5	$5000	$5000 × 1/10 = $500
6		
7		
8		
9		
10		

Fig. **5**.

Students' work showing theater owner 1's projected profit

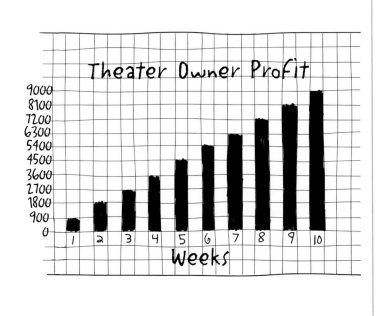

weeks, the box office receipts, and the movie distributor's and theater owner's profits. Ask the students to describe the patterns of change in the profits over the course of ten weeks (see fig. 6). Students may observe that movie distributor 1's profits increased at a constant rate of $100 each week, while theater owner 1's profit increased at a constant rate of $900 each week. Students may observe that theater owner 2's profits increase from weeks 1 through 5, but on week 6 the profits begin to decrease and actually reach $0 by week 10 ($900, $1600, $2100, $2400, $2500, $2400, $2100, $1600, $900, $0). Movie distributor 2's profits increase at a very fast rate. Help students identify these profits as square numbers: $100 ($10^2$), $400 ($20^2$), $900 ($30^2$), $1600 ($40^2$), $2500 ($50^2$), $3600 ($60^2$), $4900 ($70^2$), $6400 ($80^2$), $8100 ($90^2$), $10,000 ($100^2$).

Movie distributor 3's profits also increase but at a different rate of change. During the odd-numbered weeks, the profits increase by $200 from the previous odd-numbered week ($100, $300, $500, $700, $900). During the even-numbered weeks, the profits increase by $400 from the previous even-numbered week ($400, $800, $1200, $1600, $2000). Students may observe several interesting patterns of change for theater owner 3's profits. For instance, the profits for the even-numbered weeks increase by $1600 and are multiples of 1600 ($1600, $3200, $4800, $6400, $8000). The profits for the odd-numbered weeks increase by $1800 after week 1 and are odd multiples of 900 ($900, $2700, $4500, $6300, $8100).

Help your students renegotiate contracts

After the students discuss the patterns that they observed, give them time to plan what they are going to say when they meet to renegotiate their contracts. Then let the negotiation for new contracts begin! You may arrange the room as if it were a business conference room, with the students' desks forming a long conference table. Have each group of students present their data tables and graphs. Then have them state whether they would recommend renegotiating the contract or keeping the existing contract.

After the members of each group have presented their tables and graphs, have the class discuss which contract is the best for the theater owner and which contract is the best for the movie distributor. Then have the class discuss which contract is the best for both the theater owner and the movie distributor. The best contract is the one that will yield the greatest profit over the next five weeks. Have the student consulting teams work together to create double-bar graphs like those in figure 6, showing both the theater owner's profits and the movie distributor's profits for each of the theaters. The students can compare the profits represented on the double-bar graph as they decide which contract will yield the greatest profit for both the theater owner and the movie distributor.

As an extension to this investigation, discuss the concept of *net profit*. Provide students with an amount for the theater owners' weekly operating expenses. Then have them compute each theater owner's net profit.

To extend the investigation further, challenge the students to check their local newspaper for a report on box office receipts or consult a Web site such as the Internet Movie Database (http://www.imdb.com/boxoffice) or Lee's Movie Info (http://www.leesmovieinfo.net/BoxOffice.php) for box office receipts of currently playing movies.

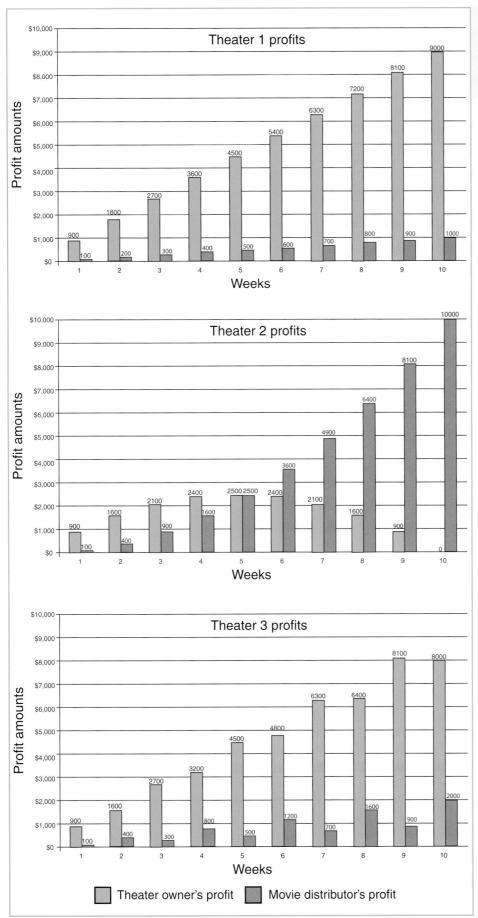

Fig. **6.**

Sample double-bar graphs showing projected profits for theaters 1, 2, and 3 (created with Microsoft Excel spreadsheet software)

The Lee's Movie Info Web site provides a movie's gross income for several days along with the total number of theaters where it is playing and the average ticket sales for each theater. A sample table of the box office gross for the movie *Shrek 2* for June 18–24, 2004, is shown here and on the CD-ROM.

Table 3.
Box Office Gross Receipts for Shrek 2, *June 18–24, 2004*

Date Playing	Box Office Gross in Millions of Dollars	Number of Theaters Where the Movie Is Playing	Average Ticket Sales per Theater
June 18	$4.156	3306	$1257
June 19	$5.398	3306	$1633
June 20	$4.388	3306	$1327
June 21	$1.887	3306	$571
June 22	$2.274	3306	$688
June 23	$1.825	3306	$552
June 24	$1.958	3306	$592

The students can graph the movie's gross receipts and its average ticket sales per theater. They can then discuss whether they would continue showing the movie on the basis of the theater's average ticket sales.

Assessment

Much of your assessment of this activity will be informal, as you observe your students organizing their data in tables and constructing bar graphs and plotting points to represent the profits over time. Giving the students an opportunity to share their mathematical explanations of the relationships that they discovered is another way to assess their ability to analyze change in various contexts.

Reflections

This investigation leads students to make connections between data displayed in charts and graphical representations and in verbal descriptions. Seeing the relationship between the variables—the change in profit over time—is key to understanding this investigation.

This activity focuses on the mathematical idea of change. After the students construct tables and graph the data, ask them to describe the relationships they see between the profits over time as well as the relationship between the profits of both the theater owners and the movie distributors. This investigation allows students to develop flexibility in their reasoning. It gives them a means of representing algebraic thinking in a real-life context as well as experience with the type of thinking that they will need for solving more complex problems. Also, the use of visual representations will strengthen the students' confidence in dealing with the mathematical idea of change—an important component in the study of algebra.

Connections

The purpose of this investigation is to help students begin to apply the idea of change and analyze change under various conditions. Understanding that many changes are predictable helps lay a foundation for applying mathematics to other fields and understanding the world. Change is an important idea that students encounter in real-life situations. For example, as part of a science unit, the students may plant seeds and record the growth of a plant. The students will be able to describe how the rate of growth varies over time as they observe and record the growth of the plant on a chart and then graph the data. These types of investigations are precursors to later work that will focus on what the slope of a line represents—that is, what the steepness of the line shows about the rate of change that is occurring.

Making and Investigating Puzzles

Focus

Reasoning about geometric relationships

Overview

This investigation helps students increase the sophistication of their reasoning about decomposing and recomposing the interiors, or areas, of two-dimensional shapes. It also encourages students to think informally about geometric concepts such as congruence and symmetry and the properties of shapes that have sides and angles.

In the first task, students investigate decomposing and recomposing rectangular areas to make and solve puzzles. In subsequent activities, students investigate and discuss how to make puzzles with geometrically stated restrictions. Students make predictions and then investigate their predictions, working either with the 2-D Shape Decomposition Tool (on the CD-ROM) or with paper, scissors, and other physical materials.

Goals

- Improve reasoning about decomposing and recomposing shapes
- Develop skill in decomposing polygonal regions and recomposing their parts to make other polygonal regions
- Move from approaching shapes strictly by visualizing them to thinking about them more analytically
- Think informally about symmetry and congruence in applied situations
- Develop ability to visualize spatial possibilities
- Use mathematics to analyze real-world situations, encouraging an appreciation for mathematics

Mathematical Content

This investigation supports the following Geometry and Process Standards and expectations for grades 3–5 (NCTM 2000, pp. 396, 402):

Geometry

- Analyze characteristics and properties of two- and three-dimensional geometric shapes and develop mathematical arguments about geometric relationships
  - Identify, compare, and analyze attributes of two- and three-dimensional shapes and develop vocabulary to describe the attributes
  - Investigate, describe, and reason about the results of subdividing, combining, and transforming shapes
  - Explore congruence

- Make and test conjectures about geometric properties and relationships and develop logical arguments to justify conclusions
  - Apply transformations and use symmetry to analyze mathematical situations
    - Predict and describe the results of sliding, flipping, and turning two-dimensional shapes
  - Use visualization, spatial reasoning, and geometric modeling to solve problems
    - Create and describe mental images of objects, patterns, and paths
    - Recognize geometric ideas and relationships and apply them to other disciplines and to problems that arise in the classroom or in everyday life

Problem Solving

- Build new mathematical knowledge through problem solving
- Solve problems that arise in mathematics and in other contexts

Reasoning and Proof

- Recognize reasoning and proof as fundamental aspects of mathematics

Decomposing the interiors of two- and three-dimensional shapes in reasoned and analytic ways is an essential intellectual skill for many types of mathematical problem solving. The development of this skill starts in the elementary grades and continues through and beyond calculus. Decomposition has many applications—for instance, finding the areas and volumes of shapes and helping students understand fractional regions. Shapes are decomposed in many applications of advanced mathematics, science, and engineering.

The decomposition concept explored in this investigation also forms a foundation for reasoning about the concept of area. Indeed, the notion of decomposition is essential for understanding that shapes that look different can have equal areas—a powerful idea that leads to the development of general methods for finding areas of nonrectangular shapes. Decomposing shapes also plays a part in understanding the properties of shapes. Such understanding is a principal component of geometric knowledge.

This investigation also encourages students to begin thinking about other essential geometric concepts such as symmetry, congruence, and transformations and classifying polygons by number of sides and angles.

Students' Mathematical Thinking

Research has produced convincing evidence that an effective way to improve mathematics instruction and learning is for teachers to understand the mathematical thought processes of their students (Fennema et al. 1996). A research-based knowledge of students' construction of meaning for core mathematical ideas can enhance teachers' understanding. For decomposing and recomposing shapes, research has identified several basic levels of sophistication in reasoning (Battista 2001).

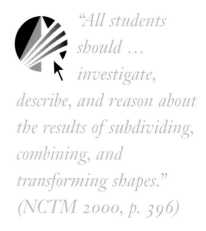

"All students should … investigate, describe, and reason about the results of subdividing, combining, and transforming shapes." (NCTM 2000, p. 396)

Decomposing the interiors of two- and three-dimensional shapes in reasoned and analytic ways is an essential intellectual skill for many types of mathematical problem solving.

Level 1: Physical Decomposing and Recomposing

At this level, students have not sufficiently abstracted the images of shapes to visualize decomposing and recomposing shapes. They have great difficulty imagining how shapes can be decomposed, so they frequently imagine decomposition inaccurately. To be successful, they must decompose and recompose shapes physically, mainly through trial and error. As students make the transition to level 2 thinking, they start to visualize possible decompositions and recompositions but must test their ideas by using concrete materials.

Level 2: Visualized Decomposing and Recomposing

Students at this level have abstracted the images of shapes well enough that they can mentally envision decomposing and recomposing them without the use of concrete materials. Students might still draw pictures to help them think about decompositions.

Level 3: Visualized Decomposing and Recomposing with the Explicit Use of Measurement

At this level, students explicitly use measurements, in addition to visualization, to decompose and recompose shapes. They determine and compare areas by using measurement-guided decomposition.

Prior Knowledge or Experience

- Using pattern blocks or putting together simple puzzles
- Informal introduction to concepts such as lines, angles, symmetry, and congruence

Materials

pp. 59; 60; 61; 62–65; 66; 67

For each student—
- A copy of each of the following blackline masters:
  - ○ "Two-Line Puzzles"
  - ○ "Three-Line Puzzles"
  - ○ "Puzzles with Special Pieces"
  - ○ "Puzzles with All Pieces Identical"
  - ○ "Dot-Paper Squares"
  - ○ "Dot-Paper Rectangles"
- A 4-by-6-inch index card for each student
- Scissors, pencils, and a ruler
- Access to the 2-D Shape Decomposition Tool (on the CD-ROM)

For the teacher—
- An overhead transparency
- An overhead projector

Classroom Environment

Throughout this investigation, the students work in pairs, and students in each pair should be approximately equal in mathematical ability.

Investigation

Making and Investigating Puzzles consists of four tasks, each with its own activity sheet. At the beginning of each task, give each student a copy of the appropriate worksheet. Pair the students and tell them that as they work on the tasks, they should discuss their thoughts with their partners. However, they should still record their own thoughts on their individual worksheets.

To progress to higher levels of thinking, students must first try to visualize the decomposition or recomposition that they need to solve each problem, then they must make a prediction, and finally they should use physical materials or the 2-D Shape Decomposition Tool on the CD-ROM to check their imagined solutions. Ask questions that encourage students to visualize solutions rather than merely use physical trial and error. For instance, as students work on the puzzles, ask, "What must a corner piece look like?" or "Could this piece fit in a corner? Make a prediction without trying the piece." As a final check, you could give the students the solutions printed from the CD-ROM or copied from the solutions section of the appendix in this book.

As the students work on these tasks, they will be able to use geometric concepts such as congruence and symmetry as well as transformations in naming and describing polygons. As they use their own language to describe these concepts, you should introduce correct geometric terminology into the discussions. For example, students might say "square corner" when describing a right angle, or they might say that pieces are *identical* when they mean *congruent*. Without saying that the students' terms are wrong, you can introduce the correct terms and have students clarify what they mean by their terms. For instance, you may ask, "How do I know what a square corner—or right angle—looks like?" A student who does not yet understand the concept of angle measure and 90-degree angles might respond that a right angle is the kind of angle she finds in the "corners" of a square or rectangle, such as the corners of her worksheet.

As the students work on a task, walk around the classroom and observe their work. Occasionally ask them to explain or justify what they are doing. If a student changes his mind about where to position a piece, ask him, "Why did you move that piece?" Carefully observe how the students are solving problems. How are they decomposing and recomposing the puzzle? Do they work strictly by trial and error, or are they reflecting before moving pieces? Do they match up pieces of the puzzle according to side lengths or angle measures? Do the students use properties of shapes to help them place puzzle pieces? For example, do they know to place pieces with right angles in the corners of the rectangle? Record your observations of students' strategies so that you can use them both for assessment and as focal points in follow-up class discussions.

After each pair of students has completed the task, have the students share their solutions, methods, and reasoning. You might record the students' solutions on an overhead transparency or chart paper and then provide time for them to verify others' solutions. Encourage students to share a wide variety of ideas, even ones that were not successful. Also, have them explain how they constructed their puzzles and how their constructed puzzles satisfy the rules and special

To progress to higher levels of thinking, students must first try to visualize the decomposition or recomposition that they need to solve each problem, then they must make a prediction, and finally they should use physical materials or the 2-D Shape Decomposition Tool on the CD-ROM to check their imagined solutions.

requirements for problems. Students' reflection on these questions will help them develop and enrich their concepts of symmetry and congruence.

Task 1: Two-Line Puzzles

Give each student a copy of the blackline master "Two-Line Puzzles." Explain that a two-line puzzle is a puzzle that is constructed by drawing two line segments on or across a rectangle to create sections that can be cut apart and used as puzzle pieces. The students make a pattern for a puzzle by drawing two straight line segments on a rectangular (4-by-6-inch) index card (see fig. 7). They must follow these rules:

- Each line segment must go from one side of the rectangle to another side.
- The line segments cannot start or end at a corner of the rectangle.

Fig. **7.**

Examples of two-line puzzles

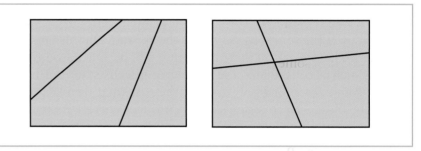

The students write their initials on each of the puzzle pieces (the initials identify their puzzles and indicate which side of the puzzle pieces is the top side). On the rectangle on their worksheets, they then draw a sketch of their puzzle. The students carefully cut apart their puzzle pieces and then mix them up. Without looking at their sketches, they then put their puzzles together. When they have finished, each student trades puzzles with his or her partner and puts the partner's puzzle together.

You can adjust the level of difficulty of these problems in a number of ways to meet the needs of your students. In general, puzzles formed by two line segments that intersect are more difficult than those formed by two line segments that do not intersect. Students who find that puzzles made with two straight line segments are not challenging enough can make puzzles with three line segments. (Three-line puzzles, however, may be too difficult for many fourth graders.) Also note that putting together puzzles with the 2-D Shape Decomposition Tool on the CD-ROM is slightly more difficult than using cutout pieces, which make physical trial and error quick and easy. Using the applet, however, makes puzzle construction more explicit and allows more reflection on the geometry of puzzles.

Some students may have difficulty assembling their partner's puzzle. Give them a blank card the size of the original rectangle and supply the following hints, one at a time:

- "Here is a copy of the original rectangle. See if you can make the puzzle on top of it."
- "Remember the rule that line segments cannot go through corners. This means that the corner pieces of the puzzle must have

at least one 'square'—or *right*—angle. So, to find a puzzle's corner pieces (and how they are positioned), look for right angles."

- "When two puzzle pieces fit next to each other, they have a common boundary. This means that each has a straight segment that is the same length. So, if two puzzle pieces have sides the same length, the pieces might fit next to each other."

- "You may look at your picture of the completed puzzle for five seconds and then you must hide it. Does looking at it first help you make your puzzle?"

If, even with these hints, the students still cannot complete a puzzle, have them put the puzzle together with the picture in front of them. Then have them cover the picture, mix up the pieces, and see if they can complete the puzzle.

Have students share their answers to the questions on the "Two-Line Puzzles" worksheet:

1. What helped you figure out how to put your partner's puzzle together?

2. What makes some student puzzles more difficult to put together than others?

3. How many triangles, quadrilaterals, pentagons, and hexagons are in your puzzle?

Task 2: Three-Line Puzzles

Hand out to each student a copy of the blackline master "Three-Line Puzzles." Using the same rules for puzzle construction as in task 1, the students make puzzles with special characteristics that connect puzzle construction to the concepts of shape, symmetry, and congruence. For each problem, the students record all the puzzles that they construct on their worksheets. Emphasize that the objective here is to analyze the decomposition of shapes by line segments, not to put together puzzles.

After the students have worked on a problem, have them share their puzzle constructions. Ask questions that specifically help them connect their reasoning to geometric ideas. For example, the first problem calls on the students to find the smallest and greatest number of pieces in a puzzle made with three line segments. Have the students describe the shapes of the pieces in puzzles having the smallest number of pieces, then the greatest. Ask questions such as the following:

- "What is special about the line segments that you use to get the fewest pieces?" (The segments do not intersect.)

- "What is special about the line segments that you use to get the most pieces?" (The segments intersect as many times as possible—that is, each segment intersects the other two segments at different points.)

Task 3: Puzzles with Special Pieces

For this task, give each student a copy of the blackline master "Puzzles with Special Pieces." These three problems use the concepts of lines of symmetry, rotational symmetry, and congruence. Let the students experiment with these puzzles.

Task 4: Puzzles with All Pieces Identical

For this task, hand out to each student a copy of the blackline master "Puzzles with All Pieces Identical." Now the students construct puzzles that have all pieces "identical" (that is, congruent). Line segments can now pass through the corners of the initial square or rectangle that students are given. Students first use one line segment, then two. As a challenge, students use cut-lines that make paths consisting of several line segments. You may have to explain to students what a "path consisting of line segments" is (the third example in fig. 8 shows a path made up of five line segments).

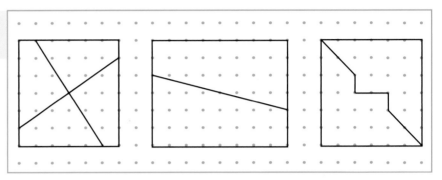

Because your students are cutting rectangles into congruent pieces, you can relate the decompositions in this activity to fractions. This is a relationship that you can easily highlight: "You cut the rectangle into four equal pieces. What fraction of the whole rectangle is each piece?"

The students work in pairs, first investigating each problem on the worksheet individually and then sharing with their partner. After they have worked on several problems, have them share their solutions with the class before continuing with subsequent problems. Seeing other students' solutions will increase their ability to imagine multiple possibilities for their puzzles.

To help your students refine their notion of "identical" pieces and incorporate this notion into the concept of congruence, ask them to prove that the parts are identical. One way to do this is to place one figure on top of another. But a more sophisticated method is to argue that corresponding sides are the same length and the corresponding angles are the same measure. Although the students may not be able to analyze angle measures, they can use the dot-paper grids or rulers to analyze side lengths. Keep in mind that two triangles are congruent if their corresponding sides are the same length. However, for two polygons that are not triangles to be congruent, the corresponding sides must be the same length and, in addition, the corresponding angles must be the same measure.

Assessment

Implementing these investigations requires you to make an ongoing assessment of your students' developing strategies and reasoning. This assessment should occur during small-group work, class discussions, and examination of the students' work.

As the students work together, listen carefully to their conversations to gather information about their reasoning and strategies. Ask questions

As the students work together, listen carefully to their conversations and ask questions that help you understand their thinking.

that help you understand their thinking. As you gather this information, relate it to the levels of student thinking described on page 26. For instance, try to ascertain whether students are visualizing correct placements of puzzle pieces before they actually place them or are merely moving the physical pieces around in a hit-or-miss fashion. Are students using length measure (by looking at dots, for example) to help them determine whether shapes that look the same actually are the same? In task 4, can students imagine possibilities without cutting out the shapes or using the computer software?

Reflections

This investigation offers students experiences in visualizing the images of shapes so that they can mentally decompose and recompose the shapes. The tasks also encourage students to make connections among such properties of shapes as side lengths and angles, decomposition of regions, congruence, symmetry, and fractions.

As students continue to do tasks like those in this investigation, they will increase their power to visualize and reason about decomposing and recomposing shapes. As they integrate those skills with their increasing knowledge of length, angle measures, properties of shapes, and other geometric concepts, they will become more proficient in their visual analyses of shapes. For instance, students will eventually be able to explain why shapes are congruent by attending to the lengths of their sides. Task 4 uses dot grids because the grids invite students to compare the measures of the sides. Such comparisons can help them decide whether two shapes are the same or how two shapes might fit together.

The geometry investigation in *Navigating through Problem Solving and Reasoning in Grade 3* (Yeatts et al. 2004) deals with decomposing and recomposing two-dimensional shapes and might serve as a resource in conjunction with activities in this investigation. The geometry investigation in *Navigating through Problem Solving and Reasoning in Grade 5* (Thompson et al., forthcoming [a]) deals with decomposing and recomposing three-dimensional areas.

Connections

Students' work on this investigation can buttress their work with fractions. Decomposing and recomposing regions are essential tasks for understanding area-region representations of fractions. (See Tierney et al. [1998] and Curcio and Bezuk [1994] for examples of such fraction activities.) Students will later apply the skills that they develop in this investigation to understanding derivations of area formulas for shapes such as triangles, parallelograms, and trapezoids. *Navigating through Problem Solving and Reasoning in Grade 6* (Thompson et al., forthcoming [b]) provides ideas to support this learning.

See Cut It Apart, Put It Together, the geometry investigation in Navigating through Problem Solving and Reasoning in Grade 3 *(Yeatts et al. 2004, pp. 19–25; 45–51), for additional ideas on teaching about decomposing and recomposing two-dimensional shapes.*

Fascinating Measures

Focus

Reasoning about measurement relationships

Overview

Elementary school students typically use both standard and nonstandard units of measure to study concepts involving length, area, perimeter, and volume. However, they need exposure to measurement concepts that arise in other contexts, such as determining one's heart rate.

In addition, students need to develop measurement sense to deal with measures that may be difficult to comprehend. For instance, the estimated apple harvest in the state of Washington for 2002 was 3.6 billion pounds of apples (http://www.bestapples.com/facts/cropfacts.html). How can students make sense of such a large measure? One strategy is to convert the total quantity to the number of pounds of apples for each person in the country. The 2002 U.S. population was approximately 280 million, so the Washington apple harvest translates to about 13 pounds of apples per person. This measure is easier for students to comprehend; a 13-pound bag of apples can be brought into the classroom and students can count the number of apples it contains. Thus, they can approximate the number of apples that the Washington apple harvest represents for each person. Students can also determine how much space they would need to store this quantity of apples for their class, their grade, and their school. As students engage in activities to help develop their measurement sense, they are also developing measurement benchmarks, or reference points, that they can use later.

Students also need to be able to convert measures from one unit to another within a measurement system. Just as they need to know how to convert from inches to feet and from meters to centimeters, they need to know how to convert from one unit of time to another. Measurement sense and measurement conversion are important concepts for students to develop in the study of measurement in the elementary grades. In this investigation, students have an opportunity to strengthen both.

As students explore mathematics, they should be encouraged to develop benchmarks for measures and use these benchmarks to make and test estimates.

Goals

- Make comparisons with measures
- Convert from one measure to another
- Evaluate the reasonableness of statements about measures

Mathematical Content

This investigation supports the following Measurement and Process Standards and expectations for grades 3–5 (NCTM 2000, pp. 398, 402).

Measurement

- Understand measureable attributes of objects and the units, systems, and processes of measurement

  ○ Carry out simple unit conversions

- Apply appropriate techniques, tools, and formulas to determine measurements
  - Select and apply appropriate standard units and tools to measure length, area, volume, weight, time, temperature, and the size of angles
  - Select and use benchmarks to estimate measurements

Problem Solving

- Build new mathematical knowledge through problem solving
- Apply and adapt a variety of appropriate strategies to solve problems

Reasoning and Proof

- Make and investigate mathematical conjectures
- Select and use various types of reasoning and methods of proof

In this investigation, students use the equivalence of two quantities—for example, 60 seconds equal 1 minute, or 12 eggs equal 1 dozen eggs—to convert a quantity from one unit of measure to another unit of measure. The actual measure does not change; the only change is in the representation of that measure.

As students convert measures, they apply problem-solving strategies to determine how to use a conversion sentence—for example, 1 foot = 12 inches. As they investigate interesting measurement claims or "facts," they discuss whether such claims are reasonable, how they can make sense of the claim, and what benchmarks are useful in understanding the measure. Finding their own interesting measurement fact and determining how to make that fact readily understandable provide another opportunity for students to reason through a process as well as justify and discuss their thinking.

Prior Knowledge or Experience

- Making simple conversions between units of measure
- Using a calculator
- Understanding the operations of multiplication and division and completing computations with a calculator

Materials

For each pair of students—

- A four-function calculator
- A stopwatch or a watch or clock with a second hand

For each student—

- A copy of each of the following blackline masters:
  - "Your Beating Heart"
  - "Eat Those Eggs"
  - "Did You Know?"

For the teacher—

- A number of interesting measurement facts to share with the class

Students need to use a variety of reasoning and problem-solving strategies as they investigate mathematics. They need to present their investigations in a form that others can evaluate and critique.

pp. 68–69; 70; 71

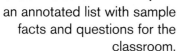

See "Web Sites for Interesting Measurements" on the CD-ROM for an annotated list with sample facts and questions for the classroom.

Before beginning the lesson, have ready a number of interesting facts or measures to pique the students' interest. One source for such facts is the book *In the Next Three Seconds…* (Morgan 1997), which the blackline masters "Your Beating Heart" and "Eat Those Eggs" call to the students' attention. Other possible sources for interesting measures are the Internet sites listed on the CD-ROM with a brief annotation and a sample fact from each.

Classroom Environment

Depending on their previous experiences, the students work in either pairs or as a class with your guidance to solve the measurement conversions and comparisons, recording their results on the appropriate blackline master. When determining their heart rate, the students work together in pairs, with one student serving as a timekeeper while the other counts the heartbeats. For the assessment, students can work individually, in pairs, or in small groups to locate their own interesting fact and then represent that fact in some other way.

Investigation

Start with an interesting measurement fact from the Internet sites on the CD-ROM or read some of the facts and measures from *In the Next Three Seconds…*, by Rowland Morgan. This book presents numerous facts and measures, predicting what might happen in the next three seconds, the next three minutes, the next three hours, and the next three days. Here are some facts from the book that students have found quite interesting:

- "In the next three seconds, the human population will increase by nine."
- "In the next three seconds, Britons will eat 3,600 potatoes."
- "In the next three minutes, Americans will eat four and a half head of cattle as take-out hamburgers."
- "In the next three minutes, people will buy 176 mobile phones."
- "In the next three hours, Americans will use paper that requires 375,000 trees to make."
- "In the next three hours, children will lose 11 hairs from their head, and these will be replaced (old folks lose 15 permanently)."

Have students predict what they could do or what could happen to them in the next three seconds. For example, some fourth-grade students thought they could do the following in the next three seconds:

- Write a word or scratch an itch
- Blink two times
- Write their name
- Turn off all the classroom lights

Then have students predict what they could do in the next three minutes. Here are some fourth-graders' predictions:

- Tie both their shoelaces
- Make a braid in their shoelaces

- Do five cartwheels
- Drink half a bottle of water
- Write a paragraph
- Sing a song

Having students think about possible activities that they can complete in three seconds or three minutes is one way to help them begin to develop benchmarks to make sense of time units. You might ask your students to try the activities that they predicted to determine their reasonableness. Making predictions and testing them are important in helping students refine their ability to make meaningful measurement estimates.

If you do not have access to *In the Next Three Seconds…*, use one of the facts from the book listed earlier or a fact from one of the Internet sites listed on the CD-ROM. Introduce these facts to generate discussions about the need to communicate and understand measures. Because most students are familiar with pizzas, using pizzas as a measure might be helpful. For instance, the Pizzaware Web site (http://www.pizzaware .com/facts.htm) reports that Americans eat about 350 large slices of pizza per second. Discuss with the students how to make this measure more understandable. Students may figure that a large pizza usually has 8 slices. To find how many whole pizzas Americans eat per second, they would divide 350 by 8 to get 43.75. So Americans eat about 44 large pizzas every second. This pizza measure is one that most students can comprehend.

Students may wonder how estimates like these in Morgan's book are made. Discuss different ways in which researchers might determine such measures and how reasonable the measures are. As a class, come back to this discussion after completing the activities for determining the reasonableness of the estimates for heart rate and eating eggs.

Have students read Rowland Morgan's prediction, included on the blackline master "Your Beating Heart," that a heart will beat about three times in the next three seconds. Most students will reason that this means their heart beats about one time per second. From this, have the students predict the number of times their heart will beat in one minute and then in one hour. To help students make reasonable estimates, have them determine the number of heartbeats for one hour, two hours, and three hours. As they see the pattern in these numbers, they should be able to estimate the number of heartbeats in one day.

According to Morgan's estimate, the heart beats about once every second, about 60 (60 × 1) times every minute, about 3600 (60 × 60) times in an hour, and about 86,400 (3600 × 24) times in a day. Help students estimate the number of heartbeats in a year. Some students may base their answer on an incorrect relationship—between the number of heartbeats in a day and the number of months in a year. Through discussion, lead the students to see that, instead, the correct relationship is between the number of heartbeats in a day (86,000) and the number of days in a year (365).

After the students have determined the heartbeats on the basis of the book's predictions, have each student determine his or her own heart rate. This is a good opportunity to talk about how such measures

Students need to create benchmarks to help them make sense of measures, including measures of time.

Americans eat about 44 large pizzas every second. (http://www.pizzaware.com/facts. htm)

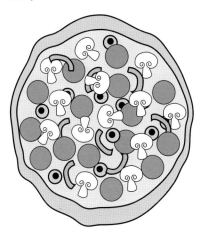

Children's literature that can complement this investigation includes Rowland Morgan's In the Next Three Seconds… *(Lodestar Books 1997) and Russell Ash's* Incredible Comparisons *(Dorling Kindersley 1996).*

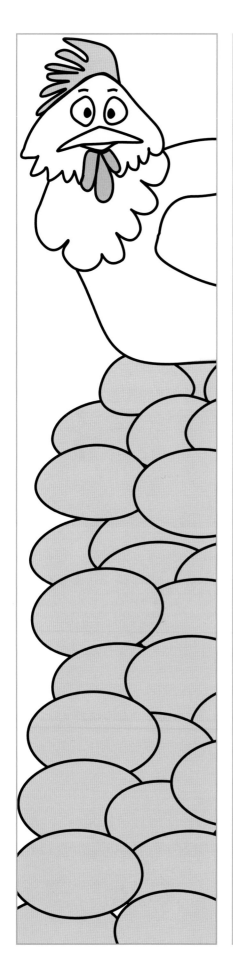

can be found. Ordinarily, we don't count the number of beats for a full minute. Instead, to estimate the heart rate for a minute, we typically find it convenient to count for 15 seconds and then multiply by 4. However, students could choose to count the number of heartbeats for different intervals of time. Encourage them to use a number of seconds that is a factor of 60 to simplify finding the number of heartbeats for a minute.

Some students are likely to need help to locate the spot near their wrist where they can detect their pulse. Have the students note their estimates for the number of times their heart beats in an hour, a day, or a year and compare these with the predictions in Morgan's book. Students should realize that heart rates vary from person to person and that their own heart rate changes according to their level of activity. To help students appreciate the number of times that their heart beats in a day, ask them to think of some other equivalent quantity. For example, students may equate the number of daily heartbeats to the number of people in a football stadium.

Ask students to guess how many years they will live and then determine the number of times their heart will beat in their predicted lifetime. If a student's heart beats 76 times per minute, it beats 4560 times per hour, 109,440 times per day, 39,945,600 times per year, and 3,195,648,000 times in a lifetime of 80 years. As an extra challenge to your students, ask students to estimate how many beats their hearts have made since they were born.

Four-function calculators may give an error message for the number of heartbeats in a lifetime because this number is beyond the capability of their display. One solution to this difficulty is to round the number of heartbeats in a year to the nearest ten million and then multiply by the number of years in a lifetime, keeping the units in millions. For the sample student's heart rate given earlier, this would mean multiplying 40 million beats in a year by 80 to obtain 3,200 million, or 3,200,000,000, heartbeats in a lifetime, which is reasonably close to the estimate obtained earlier. This approach reinforces the concept of place value with large numbers, an important topic of study for fourth-grade students.

Extension

According to Rowland Morgan's book, Americans will eat 6000 eggs in the next three seconds. To introduce the blackline master "Eat Those Eggs," ask your students, "Is this a lot of eggs in a year or not very many?" Encourage the students to convert the measure into another measure that is easier to understand or that provides a better benchmark for reasoning about measurement. When asked to think of other ways to express the measure "6000 eggs in three seconds," students may say "2000 eggs in one second," "1000 eggs in every half second," or "3000 eggs in 1.5 seconds." Still, these measures are somewhat hard to comprehend.

Some students in your class probably do not like eggs. However, remind them that eggs are an essential ingredient in a number of dishes. Eggs can be consumed in many ways, such as by eating a slice of cake or a piece of meatloaf. So an average measure needs to account for people who eat a lot of eggs as well as those who don't eat eggs as a separate dish but only as an ingredient in some food.

Students can use the processes from the blackline master "Your Beating Heart" to determine the number of eggs that Americans eat in a year (2000 eggs per second $\times$ 60 seconds per minute $\times$ 60 minutes per hour $\times$ 24 hours per day $\times$ 365 days per year = 63,072,000,000 eggs per year). Because the United States has a population of approximately 280,000,000, this is about 225 eggs, or about 19 dozen eggs, per person each year. This measure is much easier for students to visualize because they have seen a carton of a dozen eggs. In preparing for this lesson, have students bring in egg cartons from home so that you can set out 19 egg cartons on a table.

Once again, students will need to think about how to complete the computations on a four-function calculator. Here is an opportunity to connect measurement ideas with reasoning about numbers. The number of eggs eaten in a day is 172,800,000. If students try to multiply this number on their calculators by 365 days per year, they are likely to obtain an error message. However, their calculators can handle 1728 $\times$ 365, and they can then append the appropriate number of zeros. This discussion is useful in helping students learn how to use technology efficiently when a problem seems to be beyond the capabilities of the tool.

The American Egg Board (http://www.aeb.org) estimates that every American eats a little more than 21 dozen eggs each year. At a weight of 1.5 pounds per dozen for large eggs, 21 dozen eggs corresponds to about 31.5 pounds of eggs. Students can find many objects around their home or the classroom that weigh about this much. Challenge them to go beyond the questions on the blackline master by asking them if they eat about half their weight in eggs each year.

A typical egg carton for a dozen eggs is about 11 inches long by 4 inches wide by 2.5 inches high. Have the students stack 21 egg cartons together to help them visualize the volume occupied by the egg cartons holding all the eggs that one person eats each year. An interesting comparison is to stack the cartons first with the lids closed and then with the lids open so that the cartons nest inside each other.

Assessment

Much of your assessment during completion of "Your Beating Heart" and "Eat Those Eggs" will be informal. Observe as students collect data for their heart rate and as they reason to convert from one measure to another. For a more formal assessment, use the blackline master "Did You Know?" This activity sheet directs the students to find a fact about a measure that is of interest to them and then represent that measure in a meaningful way. The students' ability to reason through the multistep process of converting the unit from one expression to another gives insight into their problem-solving abilities. Students could complete this assessment individually, in pairs, or in small groups. If they work in groups, encourage them to use chart paper to record their measurement fact as well as their process of rewriting this measurement into a different form. Post these chart-paper records around the room for other groups to discuss.

The CD-ROM contains three sample responses from fourth-grade students. Student 1 was quite amazed by this fact from Morgan's book: "In the next three nights, 150 jumbo jetloads of people will starve to death." She first determined the number of jetloads of people who would starve in one night (50). With an estimate of 200 people per jet, provided by her teacher, she predicted the number of people who would starve each night (10,000), related that to the population of her school, and incorrectly concluded that this number was equivalent to 10 schools the size of hers. Her estimate was incorrect because her school's enrollment was 500 students, not the 1000 she used in her calculations. She also considered the number of people who starve to death each night (10,000) in relation to carloads of people. Estimating five people per car, she converted this figure to its equivalent in carloads—2000 carloads of people.

Student 2 used another fact from Morgan's book: "In the next three minutes, Americans will eat four and a half head of cattle as take-out hamburgers." She estimated the number of cows that would be eaten in an hour (4.5×20), a day ($4.5 \times 20 \times 24$), and a year ($4.5 \times 20 \times 24 \times 365$). She too related this number to a known quantity—her school—and predicted the number of cows that would be eaten by the students in her school (she divided the total by 500).

Student 3 was intrigued by the height of the Eiffel Tower—1052 feet—given in the book *Incredible Comparisons*. Using an estimate of the height of fourth graders—4 feet—and the fact that his class had 27 students, he determined that the total height of the students in his class, if they were stacked one on top of another, would be 108 feet. On the basis of this figure, he represented the height of the Eiffel Tower as 9 classes of students. He then multiplied 9 classes by 27 students by 9 again to obtain a total of 2187 children, which is incorrect. Notice, however, that he later determined that 9 classes of 27 students would be 243 students. If each were 4 feet tall, the total height when they were stacked would be 972 feet, a reasonably good approximation of the height of the Eiffel Tower.

Reflections

Students are fascinated by interesting facts and measures. The measures pictured in the book *In the Next Three Seconds…* capture their imagination and attention. Similarly, the interesting facts available on the Internet about common foods provide another opportunity to engage students in measurement activities that are not the norm in elementary school.

Fourth-grade students are likely to have had experience making simple conversions from one unit to another, such as from inches to feet or from minutes to hours. In this investigation, they are required to reason their way through multiple conversions. Students need to talk through this process as they move from one step to the next. For many students, the multiple-step process is not trivial. With guidance and good questioning, however, they can all be successful.

Connections

The purpose of this investigation is to help students think about measurement in unconventional situations. With the heart-rate and egg-eating activities, you and your students can make connections to science and health. Students can measure their heart rate after returning from physical education class and compare the results to those that they obtain during silent reading. Students can discuss the value of regular activity that increases heart rate. NCTM's Illuminations Web site

Students need opportunities to engage in problem-solving activities that involve multiple steps.

Navigating through Problem Solving and Reasoning in Grade 4

(http://illuminations.nctm.org/lessonplans/prek-2/heart-p2/index.html) contains a series of five activities dealing with heartbeat (based on an article by Passarello and Fennell [1992]). You may want to explore this site for additional activities and extensions related to this investigation.

This investigation connects measurement to several of the other content strands in *Principles and Standards for School Mathematics* (NCTM 2000), as well as to other disciplines. Students work with number and operations as they complete estimation computations as part of the conversion process. Further, they develop their number sense as they work with large numbers as part of the measurement process. Because students collect facts and use the facts to make measurement statements, this investigation also connects measurement to data analysis.

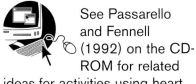

See Passarello and Fennell (1992) on the CD-ROM for related ideas for activities using heart beats.

See "The Beat of Your Heart," five lessons for grades 3–5, at the NCTM Illuminations Web Site (http://illuminations.nctm. org/index_0.aspx?id=74) for related activities.

Growing Giant Sequoias

Focus

Reasoning about data relationships

Overview

This investigation engages small groups of students in summarizing data, making a decision based on the data, and describing a procedure for making decisions in similar situations. Students are given the heights of giant sequoia seedlings grown under two different conditions, and they must decide which growing condition resulted in the tallest seedlings. They then describe their decision-making process so that they can use it again in a similar situation.

Students begin the investigation by reading about sequoias in a piece in the format of a newspaper article. They answer readiness questions as a follow-up to the article and then they learn about a hypothetical professor's work to understand that different growing conditions may enhance or retard the growth of the sequoias on the California coast. The students then analyze the professor's data. Self-assessment takes place during the problem-solving sessions within the small groups, and peer assessment occurs when groups make class presentations and peers apply the presented decision-making procedure. Teacher assessment takes place throughout the investigation.

Providing a challenging investigation to small groups of students facilitates ongoing reasoning, argument, and assessment throughout the problem-solving process.

Goals

- Use given data to decide which growing condition fosters better growth of tree seedlings

- Develop a decision-making procedure based on the data for use in future experiments

- Reevaluate and revise procedures in response to self-assessment, peer assessment, and comments made by the teacher during informal assessment.

Mathematical Content

This investigation promotes the following Data Analysis and Probability and Process Standards and expectations for grades 3–5 (NCTM 2000, pp. 400, 402):

Data Analysis and Probability
- Formulate questions that can be addressed with data and collect, organize, and display relevant data to answer them
  - Represent data using tables and graphs such as line plots, bar graphs, and line graphs

---

The development of this activity was supported by the School Mathematics and Science Center (SMSC), Purdue University, West Lafayette, Indiana, under the direction of Richard Lesh.

- Select and use appropriate statistical methods to analyze data
  - Describe the shape and important features of a set of data and compare related data sets, with an emphasis on how the data are distributed
  - Compare different representations of the same data and evaluate how well each representation shows important aspects of the data
- Develop and evaluate inferences and predictions that are based on data
  - Propose and justify conclusions and predictions that are based on data and design studies to further investigate the conclusions or predictions

Problem Solving
- Build new mathematical knowledge through problem solving
- Solve problems that arise in mathematics and other contexts
- Apply and adapt a variety of appropriate strategies to solve problems
- Monitor and reflect on the process of mathematical problem solving

Reasoning and Proof
- Make and investigate mathematical conjectures
- Develop and evaluate mathematical arguments and proofs
- Select and use various types of reasoning and methods of proof

This investigation provides opportunities for students to develop initial data-analysis concepts that are critical to making decisions with real-world data sets in scientific situations. For example, the students must make estimates for missing data, in the process encountering the notion of extrapolation. They must interpret data holistically because point-by-point comparisons do not yield the information that they need to make a decision. They have to make comparisons and interpretations to identify trends and compare two different growing conditions. Creating and articulating a decision-making procedure for interpreting the data is necessary to dealing with new sets of data.

Prior Knowledge or Experience

- Measuring centimeters to the nearest tenth (i.e., millimeters)
- Interpreting simple tables
- Computing whole and decimal numbers (either with a calculator or by hand)

Materials

For each student—
- A copy of each of the following blackline masters:
  - "Read All about It!"
  - "What Do You Now Know?"
  - "Analyzing Data for Dr. Angus"
  - "Peer Assessment Data Sets"

Developing decision-making procedures based on data is foundational to mathematical modeling, such as the creation of computer-based models for predicting the weather.

pp. 72, 73, 74, 75

- A four-function calculator
- Grid paper
- Samples of student work (available on the CD-ROM)
- Rulers
- Access to spreadsheet software (optional for graphing)

Classroom Environment

The students work in groups of three at desks or tables. The initial work by the small groups will take approximately one hour. Group presentations to the class are also an important part of the investigation.

Investigation

The blackline master "Read All about It!" presents information about giant sequoias in the format of a newspaper article. It highlights the uniqueness and importance of giant sequoia trees as well as factors that can enhance or inhibit their growth. To set the stage for this investigation, have students read the information and then complete the activity page "What Do You Now Know?" Use the students' responses to the readiness questions as a basis for a discussion of plant growth, sequoia trees, and the use of experiments involving tree seedlings.

Read aloud to the students the blackline master "Analyzing Data for Dr. Angus." This sheet describes the investigation that the students will undertake. Remind them that they must analyze data for several purposes: to compare two growing conditions, to compensate for missing data, to make a decision about Dr. Angus's set of data, and to develop a procedure, based on the data, for making decisions about future experiments. Have the students identify what they need to produce (a letter describing their decision-making procedure) and who will be using it (Dr. Angus). Tell the students that they will work in small groups to analyze the data. Then the groups will make a presentation in which they will (*a*) report their decision-making procedure for use in new experiments and (*b*) explain why their procedure will reveal any difference in the two growing conditions.

When the groups begin to work, individuals are likely to start with different ideas for estimating the missing shade data. The students will need to discuss, negotiate, and eventually decide on the procedure that they will use to estimate the missing measures. For example, in one group in another classroom, Molly suggested finding the average of the seedling heights in shade and sunlight for each day, but she didn't indicate how to use this information. Luz then built on her suggestion by saying that the group should look at the trends of growth over the weeks. The small-group setting requires students to articulate their thinking, thus revealing the development of their reasoning.

Sample Solution 1

Some students in other classrooms have used graphs of growth to make decisions; the photograph at the left shows one such student displaying her line graph.

One group first drew line graphs for the sunlight data, as illustrated in figure 9. Then the students drew line graphs for the shade data in a

Students' thinking is revealed by their dialogue when working on challenging problems in small groups, allowing excellent opportunities for teachers to assess students' reasoning.

different color on the same graph, but they had to estimate the data points for day 28, which are missing. Miguel suggested that they examine the increases from day 21 to day 28 in the sunlight to obtain the shade data. The students noticed that the seedlings in the sunlight seemed to grow faster during the first seven days, whereas the seedlings in the shade seemed to grow faster in the second seven days. The students questioned whether using the sunlight data was the best way to estimate the missing shade data. After much discussion, they simply extended the lines from the second week to the third by using the same slope as that between day 14 and day 21.

Figure 10 shows the line graphs (in blue) that the students made for the shade data by determining the data points for day 28 in this manner.

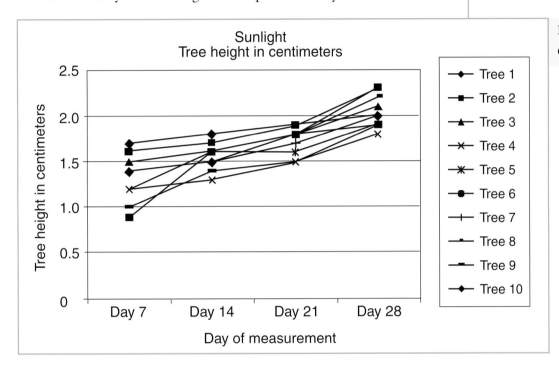

Fig. **9.**

Graph of sunlight data

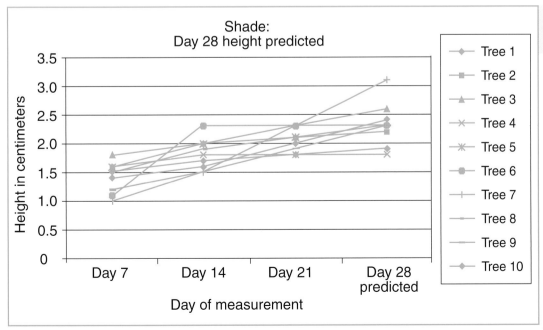

Fig. **10.**

Graph of shade data

Figure 11 shows the graphs of the sunlight data with the graphs of the shade data superimposed. Looking at the two sets of line graphs in figure 11, the students concluded that the shade condition produced taller tree seedlings because the blue line graphs as a whole extend higher than the black line graphs.

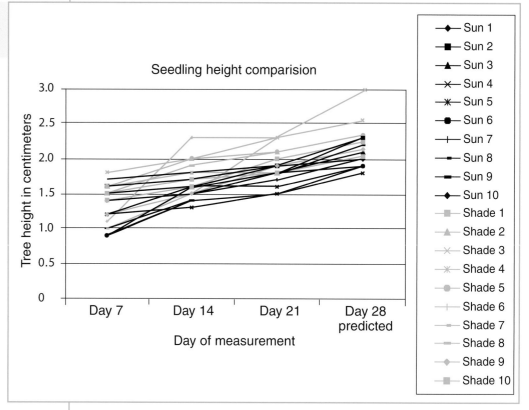

Fig. **11.**

Superimposed graphs of data for sunlight and shade

One step-by-step procedure for this approach follows:

1. Draw a black line graph of the sunlight data for each tree (days are represented on the horizontal axis; height, on the vertical axis).

2. On the same graph, draw a blue line graph of the shade data for each tree. To estimate the missing shade data, use the previous interval and assume that the increase in growth will be the same. Extend each graph by using the same slope as in the previous interval.

3. Compare the black lines with the blue lines. If the blue lines as a set seem to show more growth, then the shade condition is better. If the black lines as a set seem to show more growth, then the sun condition is better. If the two sets show about the same growth, then there is not much difference between the conditions.

Sample Solution 2

Another approach to this problem is to apply averages to the data. For example, one group of students in another classroom used the difference in heights between the previous two readings to estimate the missing shade data on day 28. They then found the average of those differences and added them to the day 21 height, as shown in

table 4. Their teacher told them that this was an appropriate way to estimate the missing data but also pointed out that they were making an assumption—that the increase in growth from day 21 to day 28 would remain the same as from day 14 to day 21.

Table 4.

A Method of Estimating Missing Shade Data for Day 28

Tree	Day 14 (cm)	Day 21 (cm)	Difference between day 14 and day 21 (cm)	Estimated day 28 (cm) (add 0.24)
1	1.7	1.8	0.1	2.04
2	2.0	2.1	0.1	2.34
3	2.0	2.3	0.3	2.54
4	1.8	1.8	0.0	2.04
5	2.0	2.1	0.1	2.34
6	2.3	2.3	0.0	2.54
7	1.5	2.3	0.8	2.54
8	1.9	2.1	0.2	2.34
9	1.5	1.9	0.4	2.14
10	1.6	2.0	0.4	2.24
Average difference between day 14 and day 21 is 2.4 ÷ 10 = 0.24 cm				

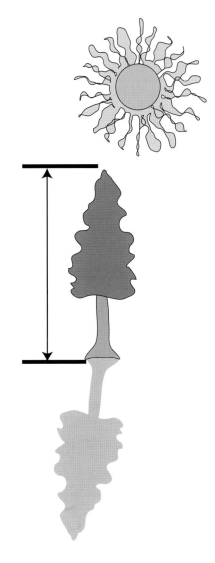

The group then found the average height for the tree seedlings on day 21. The shade data showed an average height of 2.07 centimeters, while the sunlight data showed an average height of 1.73 centimeters. The students concluded that the shade conditions resulted in taller seedlings. During the group presentation, Michael asked the group members why they had estimated the day 28 shade data if they were not going to use it in making a decision. Nicole suggested that making a comparison based on the day 28 data would be better because it was "farther out" (meaning that the group should make decisions using data closer to the final height of the trees). After hearing the class's comments, the group members revised their procedure to be consistent with the general procedure described here:

1. Estimate missing data by finding the differences between the two previous readings for all trees in the data set. Find the average of those differences. Add the average to the day 21 measures to estimate the day 28 measures.

2. Find the average for day 28 for both the sunlight data and the shade data. Compare them to decide which set of seedlings grew more. Check your conclusion by seeing if the averages for day 21, the "real" data, lead to the same conclusion.

Assessment

Group members' presentations of the letter to Dr. Angus showing their data analysis can facilitate peer assessment when classmates are

Sunlight Data for Day 21	
Tree	Height (cm)
1	1.9
2	1.9
3	1.8
4	1.5
5	1.6
6	1.8
7	1.7
8	1.8
9	1.5
10	1.8

asked to apply the group's procedure to one of the data sets on the "Peer Assessment Data Sets." You can indicate what subset of data the students should use in trying the procedures. As the students apply the presenters' procedure, ask them to comment on the clarity, completeness, and effectiveness of the presented procedure. After the presentation, have the group members revise their letter to take into account their peers' comments. You may also want to ask individual students to write a short statement about how the group's decision-making procedure was improved, thus providing an opportunity for self-assessment. You may use the group's letter for the final evaluation or as an entry in the students' portfolios. The students can evaluate the final letters by imagining themselves to be Dr. Angus asking the following questions:

- "Were the shade data extended and used?"
- "Is there a clear explanation of how the shade data were extended?"
- "Is the conclusion based on evidence that is shown and explained?"
- "Is the general decision-making procedure explained step by step so that someone else can apply the method?"

In addition to the two solutions described here, actual fourth-grade student responses, along with a discussion of each approach, are included on the CD-ROM.

Reflections

This investigation requires students to think and reason about how to extrapolate from incomplete data sets and how to combine and compare data sets in a scientific experiment. Further, they have to generalize their procedure for making a decision. Thinking and reasoning develop over the course of the investigation as students work on the problem together. A variety of ideas for estimating the missing shade data may emerge early in the session, and students may suggest overly simplistic ways to make decisions. As group members interact, they can compare, contrast, discard, or combine their ideas, resulting in more sophisticated ways of thinking. The students' reasoning develops as they are required to express their ideas, explain and defend their approach, try to understand one another's perspectives, and coordinate their ideas and knowledge to decide on an approach that is acceptable to the group. This investigation is designed to elicit peer assessment and self-assessment naturally in small-group settings in which individuals spontaneously express and test their ideas on one another and revise their thinking to reflect feedback from their peers.

Thinking and reasoning capabilities continue to develop when groups present their letters to the whole class. When classmates ask questions and provide feedback about the procedure that the group has presented, the interaction often prompts group members to reexamine and revise their approach. You can support the development of your students' reasoning when they incorporate questions and activities that require them to compare and contrast their own approaches with those of other groups. Understanding the strengths, weaknesses, and trade-offs of different sets of procedures leads to further cycles of assessment and revision, enhancing the development of students' thinking and reasoning.

Two types of misconceptions have surfaced in this investigation. One type relates to the broad class of complex problems that have more than one correct response and that require problem formulation—that is, the problem solvers have to figure out what mathematical questions they need to answer. Two examples are given here:

- Students may expect an investigation to conclude with only one correct method for making a decision. If so, they may become frustrated. They may resist engaging in the problem or feel at a loss because the problem formulation required in the investigation seems overwhelming. To help students overcome this misconception, emphasize that there are a number of good ways to work through this investigation and that real-world scientific experiments often have a number of good methods for making final recommendations. In this investigation, the students could use multiple representations—tables, graphs, and charts—to display the data to support their final decision. Working in small groups also helps students persevere and stay engaged.

- Students may expect to identify and use a decision-making approach that they have been previously taught. Students who have had limited experience with problems that require them to go through multiple cycles of expressing, testing, and revising their ideas may be frustrated when they find that they need to modify their initial method of analyzing the data repeatedly during the collaborative problem-solving process. Although initial solutions to problems are posed, tested, and modified frequently in everyday life, students are often surprised to find this process occurring in mathematics class. Assure your students that revising and modifying their initial ideas are activities that you expect and that are also good for their learning. As students engage in more investigations like these, they will begin to recognize that cycles of revision are a natural and constructive part of the problem-solving process.

The second type of misconception specifically relates to the content of the investigation. Two examples follow:

- Students may find the average of all the values in each figure and table without considering the fact that the measurements were taken on different days. They may be computing simply for the sake of computing. In addition, unlike in many other types of problems, they must sort the information given.

- Students who have never compared data sets of different sizes may compare wrong or dissimilar data. For example, students may compare the shade data for day 21 to the sunlight data for day 28. Even though the figures and tables are labeled with different days and the problem statement mentions the distinction in the data sets, students may still try to compare the last column in one with the last column in another.

Connections

This investigation supports connections to both science (the study of plants and scientific experimentation) and language arts (written and spoken presentations). It engages students in data analysis, problem

solving, and reasoning. During the small-group presentations to the whole class, when students apply other groups' approaches, they have opportunities to use different kinds of representations (graphs and tables), engage in different kinds of data analysis (graphical analyses, analyses that use averages), and work with different kinds of numbers (whole numbers and decimals). The notion of *generalization*, not commonly incorporated in fourth-grade curricula, comes into play when the students apply the groups' procedures to new data sets. This investigation also opens the door to related activities that can help students develop their use of statistical decision making. Two possibilities follow:

- Present the sample student solutions on the CD-ROM.
  - Ask the students to rank the sample solutions from the most satisfactory to the least satisfactory. Discuss the strengths and weaknesses of each solution.
  - Ask the students to write a letter to a small group on behalf of Dr. Angus, making suggestions for improving the group's clarity, completeness, or method.
- Decide on an experiment that the students can conduct in class (see fig. 12). Ask them to make a decision about the outcome. Then have them write a general procedure for analyzing the data and drawing conclusions for other sets of data.

Using data analysis to make decisions and create data-based procedures for making those decisions are important aspects of scientific study. Using statistics in these ways helps students begin to build the foundations that they will need as informed citizens in the future. Even fourth-grade students can begin to engage in these kinds of investigations, developing the intuitions that undergird the statistics and probability concepts taught in secondary- and collegiate-level courses. Further, such investigations give students a chance to apply their knowledge of numbers and engage in problem solving and reasoning in new and interesting ways, stretching their thinking to develop mathematical approaches that they can remember and reuse in the future.

See Navigating through Data Analysis and Probability in Grades 3–5 *(Chapin et al. 2003) for more ideas for incorporating statistics into the curriculum.*

Fig. 12.

Questions for classroom-based experiments

- Will plants grow better in the shade of a counter or by a sunny window in the classroom?
- Do right-handed students consistently fold their hands with their left thumb over the right thumb though left-handed students consistently fold their hands with their right thumb over their left thumb?
- Do students who walk to school leave home earlier in the morning than students who ride a bus?
- Do students who watch one-half hour or less of television a day read more than students who watch more than one-half hour of television a day?
- Do plants that receive a lot of water grow faster than plants that receive only a little water?
- Do students who bring lunch to school eat more fruits and vegetables than students who buy lunch at school?
- Do students in the fourth grade read the same number of books each week as students in the fifth grade?

PROBLEM SOLVING *and* REASONING

Looking Back and Looking Ahead

The investigations in this book emphasize problem solving and reasoning in the five content strands of the mathematics curriculum—number and operations, algebra, geometry, measurement, and data analysis and probability. The explorations were designed to stimulate students to think and reason while solving interesting problems.

Problem solving is the cornerstone of all school mathematics, prekindergarten–grade 12. Concepts and computational skills are not very useful if they are not accompanied by the ability to solve problems. A student who can divide accurately but cannot recognize a situation that calls for division is very limited as a problem solver.

The goal of all school mathematics is to enable students to use facts, concepts, and procedures to solve increasingly challenging problems as they progress in school. Students in grades 3–6 should have daily experiences with problems that interest them and challenge them to think about various ideas in mathematical contexts. Good problems and problem-solving situations encourage both reasoning and communication. They stimulate students to exchange ideas with one another and with their teachers. These experiences also challenge students to develop and apply strategies, introduce them to new concepts, and provide a context for applying the skills that they have learned.

Teachers can help students become good problem solvers by selecting appropriate problems, giving students time to think and develop solution strategies, encouraging them to discuss their ideas, and assessing their understanding of the mathematics involved. Because good problems are challenging, students may encounter difficulty in arriving at solutions. Teachers must decide when their own input is necessary and when it is not. It is important for teachers and students to realize that challenging problems take time to solve and that perseverance is necessary.

Students in grades 3–6 are poised to make important transitions in their reasoning. Until this time, many students have believed that something is always true if they have seen one or more examples of it. Now students learn that several examples are not sufficient to establish the general truth of a conjecture, and they discover that a single counterexample can show that a conjecture is not true.

Upper elementary students also need to learn what constitutes an acceptable explanation. Teachers must encourage them to explain and justify their thinking and help them learn how to detect fallacies in other students' thinking. Students should also move from considering individual mathematical objects (*this* triangle) to thinking about classes of objects (*all* triangles).

The process of problem solving and reasoning is not learned at any particular grade level but unfolds, deepens, and grows each year. As students enter the middle grades, they should bring a sound foundation on which they can build mathematics that is more challenging than any they have encountered before.

All mathematics educators aim to teach more mathematics and to teach it better. To do so, they must model good problem-solving strategies and exhibit logical reasoning in the classroom. Students whose teachers are exemplary role models will be positively disposed toward mathematics.

NAVIGATIONS SERIES

GRADE 4

PROBLEM SOLVING *and* REASONING

Appendix

Blackline Masters and Solutions

Using the Sieve of Eratosthenes

Name _____

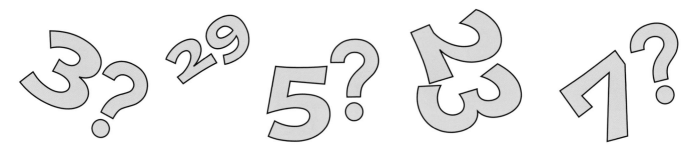

How many prime numbers do you think exist between 1 and 100? You can explore this question by using the Sieve of Eratosthenes to sift through the numbers. You'll need a hundreds chart from your teacher for your sieve.

1. Cross off the number 1 on your chart because it is not prime. Remember that a prime number has exactly two factors—itself and 1—and the factors must be different from each other.

2. Circle the number 2 in green. It has exactly two factors—itself and 1—so it is a prime. Use green to cross off all the multiples of 2 on your chart. Each of these numbers has at least three factors—1, 2, and the number itself—so none of the multiples of 2 is a prime.

   a. Look at the pattern that the crossed-off numbers make on the chart. Does the pattern help you discover anything about the numbers that are multiples of 2?

   b. Can you come up with a rule about the numbers that you can divide evenly by 2?

3. Now circle the number 3 in red. It has exactly two factors—itself and 1—so it is a prime. Use red to cross off all the multiples of 3. Each of these numbers has at least three factors—1, 3, and the number itself—so none of the multiples of 3 is a prime. You may discover that you have already crossed off some of the multiples of 3 in green. If this is so, cross them off again in red.

   a. Look at the pattern of crossed-off numbers on your chart now. Does the pattern help you discover anything about the numbers that are multiples of 3? (*Hint:* Consider the number 6. You have crossed it off in both red and green. This means that 6 has both 2 and 3 as factors, so 6 is a multiple of both 2 and 3.)

   b. Can you come up with a rule about numbers that you can divide evenly by 3?

Navigating through Problem Solving and Reasoning in Grade 4

Name _____

4. On your chart you have already crossed off the number 4 (because it is a multiple of 2), so move to the number 5. Circle the 5 in blue. It is another prime because it also has exactly two factors—itself and one. Use blue to cross off all the multiples of 5. Each of these numbers has at least three factors. If you have already crossed off any of these numbers in green or red, cross it off again in blue.

    a. Look at the pattern of crossed-off numbers on your chart now. Does the pattern help you discover anything about the numbers that are multiples of 5?

    b. Can you come up with a rule about numbers that you can divide evenly by 5?

5. Repeat the process that you have been following for circling prime numbers and crossing off numbers that are multiples. Use a different color each time, and continue working until your chart has no numbers left for you to cross off or circle.

    a. Write down any discoveries that the color patterns help you make.

    b. List any rules that you come up with about numbers that you can divide evenly by a particular prime number.

6. How many prime numbers have you managed to "catch" in your sieve? _____ List them.

Hundreds Chart

1	2	3	4	5	6	7	8	9	10
11	12	13	14	15	16	17	18	19	20
21	22	23	24	25	26	27	28	29	30
31	32	33	34	35	36	37	38	39	40
41	42	43	44	45	46	47	48	49	50
51	52	53	54	55	56	57	58	59	60
61	62	63	64	65	66	67	68	69	70
71	72	73	74	75	76	77	78	79	80
81	82	83	84	85	86	87	88	89	90
91	92	93	94	95	96	97	98	99	100

Movie Money Matters

Name _____

Contract for Theater Owner 1

I agree to pay the Movie Distributor one-tenth of the total box office receipts each week.

Contract for Theater Owner 2

I agree to pay the Movie Distributor one-tenth of the box office receipts for the first week, two-tenths for the second week; three-tenths for the third week; four-tenths for the fourth week; and five-tenths for the fifth week.

Contract for Theater Owner 3

I agree to pay the Movie Distributor one-tenth of the box office receipts for the odd-numbered weeks and two-tenths of the box office receipts for the even-numbered weeks.

Box Office Receipts	
Week 1	$1000
Week 2	$2000
Week 3	$3000
Week 4	$4000
Week 5	$5000

Movie Distributor's Profit

Name _____

Movie Distributor's Profit from Theater _____		
Week	Box Office Receipts	Movie Distributor's Profit

Navigating through Problem Solving and Reasoning in Grade 4

Theater Owner's Profit

Name _____

Theater Owner _____			
Week	Box Office Receipts	Amount Paid to Movie Distributor	Theater Owner's Profit

Centimeter Grid Paper

Name _____

Two-Line Puzzles

Name _____

1. Make a pattern for a puzzle by drawing two straight lines on a rectangular (4-by-6-inch) index card. You must follow these rules:
   - Your line segments must go from one side of the rectangle to another side.
   - Your line segments cannot start or end at a corner of the rectangle.

2. Write your initials on the face of each of the puzzle pieces (Your initials will identify your puzzle and let you know which side of the puzzle pieces should be showing.)

3. Draw a sketch of your puzzle on the rectangle at the bottom of the page. Fold your sketch back so that you cannot see it.

4. Using the 4-by-6-inch index card, carefully cut your puzzle pieces apart and then mix them up. Put your puzzle together without looking at your sketch.

5. Trade puzzles with a partner and put your partner's puzzle together.

   a. What helped you figure out how to put your partner's puzzle together?

   b. What makes some puzzles more difficult to put together than others?

6. How many triangles are in your puzzle? _____ How many quadrilaterals? _____ How many pentagons? _____ How many hexagons?_____

Fold back on this line

Three-Line Puzzles

Name _____

1. Make a pattern for a puzzle by drawing three straight lines on a rectangular (4-by-6-inch) index card. You must follow these rules:
   - Your line segments must go from one side of the rectangle to another side.
   - Your line segments cannot start or end at a corner of the rectangle.

2. What is the smallest number of pieces that a three-line puzzle can have? _____ What is the greatest number of pieces that a three-line puzzle can have? _____ Draw examples of your answers.

smallest number   *greatest number*

3. Make a three-line puzzle with no triangles.

4. Make a three-line puzzle with three triangles and one quadrilateral.

5. Make a three-line puzzle that has all quadrilateral pieces.

Navigating through Problem Solving and Reasoning in Grade 4

Puzzles with Special Pieces

Name _____

1. Make a two-line or three-line puzzle and put your initials on all the pieces. Make your puzzle so that it has a piece that fits two ways: (1) when the piece is face up (so your initials are showing) and (2) when the piece is flipped over, or face down (so your initials are not showing). What is special about this piece?

2. Make a two-line or three-line puzzle that has a piece that fits in two or more ways. In each way, however, your initials must be showing. What is special about this piece?

3. Make a two-line or three-line puzzle that has two pieces that can be traded and still fit. What is special about these pieces?

Puzzles with All Pieces Identical

Name _____

1. Use one straight line to cut a 6-by-6-unit square into two identical pieces. How many different ways can you find to do this? _____ Record your solutions below. (Cuts can start and stop in corners of the square. Cuts must start and stop at dots.)

Navigating through Problem Solving and Reasoning in Grade 4

Name _____

2. Use one straight line segment to cut a 6-by-8-unit rectangle into two identical pieces. How many different ways can you find to do this? _____ Record your solutions below. (Cuts can start and stop in corners of the square. Cuts must start and stop at dots.)

3. Use two straight lines to cut a 6-by-6-unit square into four identical pieces. How many different ways can you find to do this? _____ Record your solutions below. (Cuts can start and stop in corners of the square. Cuts must start and stop at dots.)

4. Use as many straight lines as you wish to cut a 6-by-8-unit rectangle into four identical pieces. (The lines must still start and end on the sides of the rectangle.) How many different ways can you find to do this? _____ Record your solutions below. (Cuts can start and stop in corners of the square. Cuts must start and stop at dots.)

Challenge Problem

Use two "zigzag" paths consisting of two or more lines to cut a 6-by-6-unit square or a 6-by-8-unit rectangle into four identical pieces. Record each cut on a worksheet (Dot-Paper Squares or the Dot-Paper Rectangles). (Cuts can start and stop in corners of the square. Cuts must start and stop at dots.)

Dot-Paper Squares

Name _____

Dot-Paper Rectangles

Name _____

Your Beating Heart

Name _____

Many interesting facts rest on measurements. Here is one interesting fact about your body. Your heart will beat about three times in the next three seconds. This is what Rowland Morgan claims in his book *In the Next Three Seconds*…. Use his predictions to answer questions 1–4. Be sure to show your work and explain how you got your answer.

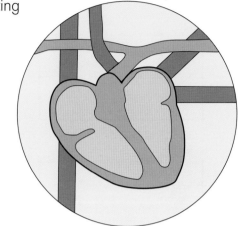

1. If your heart beats three times in the next three seconds, how many times will your heart beat in a minute?

2. How many times will your heart beat in an hour?

3. How many times will your heart beat in a day?

4. How many times will your heart beat in a year?

5. Check your heart rate. To find your pulse, hold your first two fingers on your wrist just below your palm.

   a. To find the number of times your heart beats in a minute, do not count for a whole minute. Instead, have your partner time you for 15 seconds while you count the number of times your heart beats.

   b. How can you use the number of times your heart beats in 15 seconds to find the number of times your heart beats in a minute?

Name _____

c. Use your answers from (*a*) and (*b*). Compare your heart rate with the value predicted by Rowland Morgan in question 1.

d. Find the number of times your heart beats in a day.

e. Where else can you find a number this great?

6. Your heart rate changes depending on your level of physical activity. Compare your heart rate after sitting still to your heart rate after physical education class.

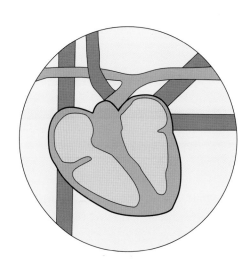

Eat Those Eggs

Name _____

There are many interesting facts about life in the United States and in the world. Sometimes the facts are difficult to understand. So it often is helpful to change the measurements into other ones that are easier to understand. In his book *In the Next Three Seconds…*, Rowland Morgan claims that Americans will eat 6000 eggs in the next three seconds.

1. What are some other ways in which you could think about this fact?

2. Using Morgan's prediction, about how many dozen eggs will every American eat in a year?

3. According to the American Egg Board, the average number of eggs that each person ate in 2001 was 259.7. Compare this figure with Morgan's prediction.

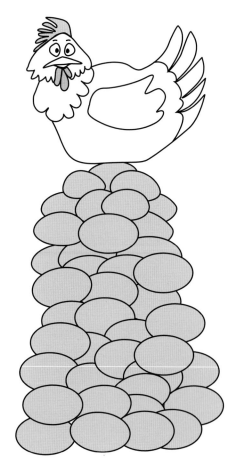

4. A dozen large eggs weigh about 1.5 pounds.

   a. How many pounds of eggs does a typical American eat in a year?

   b. What else weighs about this much? How do you know?

5. Use an egg carton to think about the space that the eggs eaten by each American in a year would occupy.

   a. Estimate the volume of a single egg carton. Measure its length, width, and height.

   b. If you stacked all the egg cartons for one person on top of one another, what would the estimated volume be?

Did You Know?

Name _____

1. Find your own fascinating measurement fact. Write it here and tell where you found it.

2. Change your fact in some way to make it easier to understand. Show how you changed your fact.

3. Use your work from step 2 to rewrite your fact in a different form.

Name _____

Giant Sequoia Trees

Giant sequoia trees are some of the largest and oldest living things on earth. In fact, the "General Sherman" giant sequoia tree in Sequoia National Park in California is the largest tree by volume in the world. When measured in 1975, the tree was a little more than 52.5 cubic feet and almost 275 feet tall. Sequoia trees grow to 361 feet. The huge trees are valuable to loggers because the wood is very strong and resistant to decay. Coastal sequoias are good for building houses and furniture. The wood is also very beautiful. Because it is so useful, many of the trees were cut down in the early 1900s.

However, old sequoias are also valuable to the environment because many different kinds of animals and insects live in them. Even fallen sequoia trees provide homes and food for animals and plants in the forest. Because it takes a long time for the wood to decay, animals or groups of insects can live in the trees for many years. The decaying trees can also help new sequoia trees grow. The sequoia tree plays an important role in the environment from seedling until long after the aged tree falls over.

Sequoias can live for hundreds of years and grow to be very wide and tall. Their roots do not grow very far under the surface, allowing sequoias to absorb as much water as possible. Because their roots are so shallow, the trees need to grow in clusters to help them stand up. If they grew alone, they might fall down, because they can become so big. The seedlings also need to grow tall very quickly to reach the sunlight in a dense forest.

Scientists are still trying to understand how sequoia trees can become so big and why they live for so long. Scientists would also like to grow more sequoias in the greenhouse so that they can replant them back in the forest.

What Do You Now Know?

Name _____

1. Why is the sequoia tree important to the environment?

2. Why are the roots of the sequoia so shallow?

3. What are some things tree seedlings might need to grow well?

Analyzing Data for Dr. Angus

Name _____

Tree growers in California want to improve the growth of coastal sequoia trees. They are trying to decide what conditions are best for growing sequoia trees in the greenhouse.

To help the growers make their decision, Dr. Wendy Angus grew coastal sequoia seedlings under two different conditions. She is testing two different types of light: white light and far-red light. White light is like bright sunlight. Far-red light simulates shade in the greenhouse. She would like to know which type of light helps the seedlings grow tall more quickly.

Dr. Angus grew ten plants in each type of light. On day 22, one of the lab assistants knocked over the seedlings grown in the shade, and all the seedlings fell out of their pots. So she measured the trees grown in the shade only on day 7, day 14, and day 21. She measured the trees grown in the sunlight on day 7, day 14, day 21, and day 28. Despite the accident in the lab, Dr. Angus would still like to use the data she has collected.

Original Data Set

Sunlight (Tree height in centimeters)					Shade (Tree height in centimeters)			
Tree	Day 7	Day 14	Day 21	Day 28	Tree	Day 7	Day 14	Day 21
1	1.7	1.8	1.9	2.0	1	1.5	1.7	1.8
2	1.6	1.7	1.9	2.3	2	1.6	2.0	2.1
3	1.5	1.6	1.8	2.1	3	1.8	2.0	2.3
4	1.2	1.3	1.5	1.8	4	1.6	1.8	1.8
5	0.9	1.6	1.6	1.9	5	1.6	2.0	2.1
6	0.9	1.6	1.8	1.9	6	1.1	2.3	2.3
7	1.4	1.5	1.7	2.0	7	1.0	1.5	2.3
8	1.2	1.6	1.8	2.2	8	1.5	1.9	2.1
9	1.0	1.4	1.5	1.9	9	1.2	1.5	1.9
10	1.4	1.5	1.8	2.3	10	1.4	1.6	2.0

Your Letter

After analyzing the data above, write a letter explaining to Dr. Angus how to decide which type of light is better for helping coastal sequoia seedlings grow. Describe the method you used to analyze the data so that she can use it for other data sets in similar conditions.

Peer Assessment Data Sets

Name _____

As your peers present their decision-making procedures, test them by applying them to some data. Your teacher will tell you which data to use. As you apply a procedure, think of questions to ask and suggestions to make to the presenters. The goal is to help the presenters clarify and improve their procedure.

Data Set 2

Sunlight (Tree height in centimeters)				
Tree	Day 7	Day 14	Day 21	Day 28
Tree 1	1.2	1.7	1.8	2.2
Tree 2	1.4	1.6	1.9	2.3
Tree 3	1.5	1.7	2.1	2.3
Tree 4	1.3	1.5	1.8	2.3
Tree 5	1.0	1.6	2.0	2.1
Tree 6	0.9	1.1	2.3	2.3
Tree 7	0.9	1.0	1.5	2.3
Tree 8	1.2	1.5	1.9	2.1
Tree 9	1.0	1.4	1.7	2.3
Tree 10	1.1	1.4	1.6	2.0.

Shade (Tree height in centimeters)			
Tree	Day 7	Day 14	Day 21
Tree 1	1.2	1.4	1.8
Tree 2	1.5	1.7	2.1
Tree 3	1.5	1.6	1.8
Tree 4	1.6	1.8	2.1
Tree 5	1.0	1.5	1.6
Tree 6	0.9	1.6	1.8
Tree 7	1.1	1.3	1.7
Tree 8	1.2	1.5	1.8
Tree 9	1.0	1.4	1.5
Tree 10	1.4	1.5	1.8

Data Set 3

Sunlight (Tree height in centimeters)				
Tree	Day 7	Day 14	Day 21	Day 28
Tree 1	1.2	1.4	1.8	2.0
Tree 2	1.5	1.7	2.1	2.3
Tree 3	1.5	1.6	1.8	2.2
Tree 4	1.2	1.3	1.5	1.8
Tree 5	1.0	1.5	1.6	1.9
Tree 6	0.9	1.6	1.8	2.0
Tree 7	1.1	1.3	1.7	2.1
Tree 8	1.2	1.5	1.8	2.2
Tree 9	1.0	1.4	1.5	1.9
Tree 10	1.4	1.5	1.8	2.3

Shade (Tree height in centimeters)			
Tree	Day 7	Day 14	Day 21
Tree 1	1.7	1.8	2.2
Tree 2	1.6	1.9	2.1
Tree 3	1.7	2.1	2.3
Tree 4	1.5	1.8	2.3
Tree 5	1.6	2.0	2.1
Tree 6	1.1	2.3	2.3
Tree 7	1.0	1.5	2.3
Tree 8	1.5	1.9	2.1
Tree 9	1.4	1.7	1.9
Tree 10	1.4	1.6	2.0

Solutions for the Blackline Masters

Solutions for "Using the Sieve of Eratosthenes"

Students' answers will vary in response to the questions about what the patterns reveal to them and what rules they can find; figure 2 and the discussion of the activity in the text provide possible responses. (See pp. 11–12.)

The prime numbers between 1 and 100 are 2, 3, 5, 7, 11, 13, 17, 19, 23, 29, 31, 37, 41, 43, 47, 53, 59, 61, 67, 71, 73, 79, 83, 89, and 97.

Solutions for "Movie Distributor's Profit" and "Theater Owner's Profit"

The following chart shows the profit for both the movie distributors and the theater owners for each contract:

Week	Box Office Receipts	Contract 1	Movie Distributor's Profit from Contract 1	Theater Owner's Profit from Contract 1	Contract 2	Movie Distributor's Profit from Contract 2	Theater Owner's Profit from Contract 2	Contract 3	Movie Distributor's Profit from Contract 3	Theater Owner's Profit from Contract 3
1	$1000	1/10	$100	$900	1/10	$100	$900	1/10	$100	$900
2	$2000	1/10	$200	$1800	2/10	$400	$1600	2/10	$400	$1600
3	$3000	1/10	$300	$2700	3/10	$900	$2100	1/10	$300	$2700
4	$4000	1/10	$400	$3600	4/10	$1600	$2400	2/10	$800	$3200
5	$5000	1/10	$500	$4500	5/10	$2500	$2500	1/10	$500	$4500
6	$6000	1/10	$600	$5400	6/10	$3600	$2400	2/10	$1200	$4800
7	$7000	1/10	$700	$6300	7/10	$4900	$2100	1/10	$700	$6300
8	$8000	1/10	$800	$7200	8/10	$6400	$1600	2/10	$1600	$6400
9	$9000	1/10	$900	$8100	9/10	$8100	$900	1/10	$900	$8100
10	$10000	1/10	$1000	$9000	10/10	$10000	$0	2/10	$2000	$8000

Sample work by students, including computer-generated graphs, appears on the CD-ROM.

Navigating through Problem Solving and Reasoning in Grade 4

Solutions for "Two-Line Puzzles"

1–4. (Steps in the process of making a puzzle.)

5. Students' responses will vary.

6. Two-line puzzles that follow the rules in the activity can have 0–2 triangles, 0–4 quadrilaterals, 0–2 pentagons, and 0–1 hexagons. The following table and corresponding examples show the possibilities. Other dissections are possible.

	Possible Combinations							
	A	B	C	D	E	F	G	H
Triangles	0	0	1	1	2	2	2	1
Quadrilaterals	4	3	2	1	0	0	0	2
Pentagons	0	0	1	1	2	0	1	0
Hexagons	0	0	0	0	0	1	0	0
Total pieces	4	3	4	3	4	3	3	3

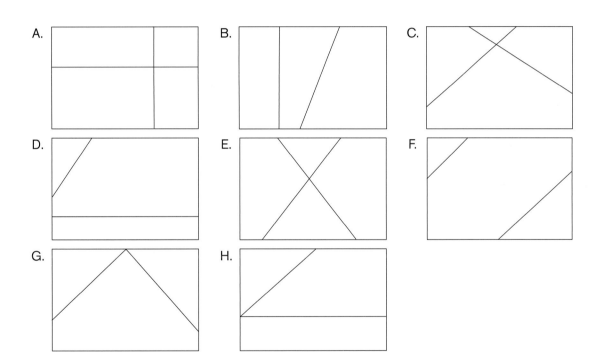

Solutions for "Three-Line Puzzles"

2. The smallest number of pieces is 4. The greatest number of pieces is 7. Samples are shown.

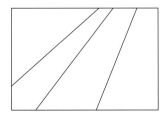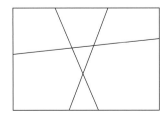

3. One sample solution is shown below.

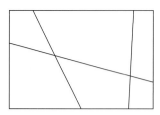

4. One sample solution is shown below.

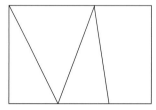

5. One sample solution is shown below.

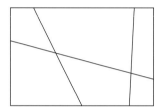

Solutions for "Puzzles with Special Pieces"

1. A puzzle piece will fit both face up (i.e., so the initials are showing) and face down only if it has at least one line of symmetry. (All the pieces in sample puzzle 1 fit face up and face down because each has at least one line of symmetry.)

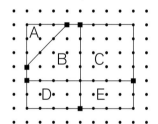

Sample puzzle 1

2. A puzzle piece fits face up in a puzzle in several ways if it has rotational symmetry. (In sample puzzle 1, piece C can be turned four different ways to fit in the puzzle face up. Pieces D and E can each fit two different ways.)

3. Two puzzle pieces are interchangeable if they are congruent. (In sample puzzle 1, pieces D and E are interchangeable because they are congruent.) In sample puzzle 2, one piece can be flipped and still fit (A), one piece can be rotated and still fit (B), and two pieces can be interchanged and still fit (C and D).

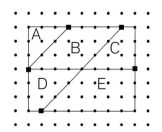

Sample puzzle 2

Solutions for "Puzzles with All Pieces Identical"

Recall that cuts must go from dot to dot.

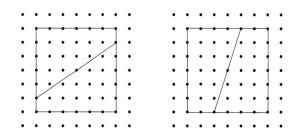

1. Students might use the vertical or horizontal cuts connecting the midpoints of opposite sides of the square. They might also use diagonal cuts. The additional solutions shown at the right are less obvious but still divide the square into two congruent pieces.

2. Students might use the vertical or horizontal cuts connecting the midpoints of opposite sides of the rectangle. They might also use diagonal cuts. The additional solutions shown below are less obvious but still divide the rectangle into two congruent pieces.

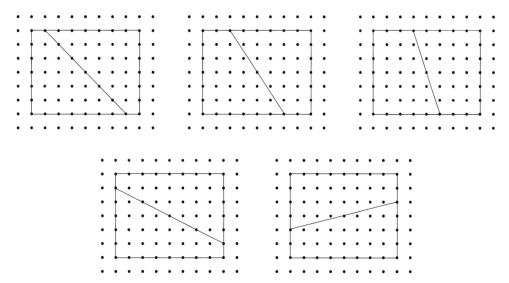

3. Students may easily find the vertical and horizontal cuts through the midpoints of each side of the square dividing it into four congruent squares. Another solution is to draw both diagonals from corner to corner making four triangles. Two other solutions are shown below.

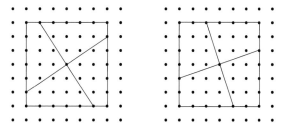

4. Sample solutions for cutting a rectangle into four congruent pieces appear below.

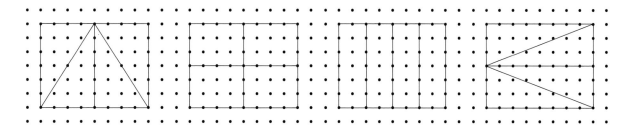

Challenge Problem

Examples of two multisegment paths that cut a square into four congruent pieces are shown below.

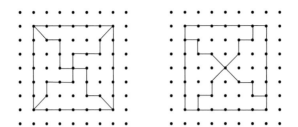

Solutions for "Your Beating Heart"

1. In his book *In the Next Three Seconds…*, Rowland Morgan claims that the heart beats 60 times per minute. If the heart beats three times in three seconds, then it beats one time in one second. Because there are 60 seconds in a minute, this means that there are 60 heartbeats in a minute.

2. 3600 times. There are 60 minutes in an hour, so the students should multiply the number of times the heart beats in a minute by the number of minutes in an hour: $60 \times 60 = 3600$. They should notice that the units work out. (60 heartbeats per minute × 60 minutes per hour = 3600 heartbeats per hour)

3. 86,400 times. There are 24 hours in a day, so the students should multiply the number of times the heart beats in an hour by the number of hours in a day: $3600 \times 24 = 86,400$. (3600 heartbeats per hour ×24 hours per day = 86,400 heartbeats per day)

4. 31,536,000 times. There are 365 days in a year, so the students should multiply the number of times the heart beats in a day by the number of days in a year: $86,400 \times 365 = 31,536,000$. (86,400 heartbeats per day × 365 days per year = 31,536,000 heartbeats per year)

5. *a.* Answers will vary.
   b. Because $15 \times 4 = 60$, students can multiply the number of times their heart beats in 15 seconds by 4 to find the number of times that it beats in a minute.
   c. Answers will vary. A person's heart rate when sitting still is likely to be between 70 and 80 beats per minute.
   d. To find the number of times that his or her heart beats in a day, a student can first find the number of times that it beats in an hour and then the number of times that it beats in a day, replicating the work in problems 2 and 3. Answers will vary. For a heart rate of 75 beats per minute, the heart would beat $75 \times 60 = 4500$ times in an hour and $4500 \times 24 = 108,000$ times in a day.
   e. Responses will vary. Samples might include about 1.5 large football stadiums full of people or the population of a small city

6. Responses will vary. The heart rate is likely to be higher after physical activity than after sitting still.

Solutions for "Eat Those Eggs"

1. Responses will vary. Students might think of 6000 eggs in 3 seconds as equivalent to 2000 eggs per second, 3000 eggs in 1.5 seconds, or 120,000 eggs in 1 minute.

2. If Americans eat 6000 eggs in 3 seconds, then they eat 120,000 eggs in 1 minute. They also eat 120,000 eggs per minute × 60 minutes per hour = 7,200,000 eggs in an hour. This becomes $7,200,000 \times 24 = 172,800,000$ eggs in a day. In a year, then, Americans eat $172,800,000 \times 365 = 63,072,000,000$ eggs. Because the population of the United States is about 280,000,000, this means that each American consumes about $63,072,000,000 \div 280,000,000 = 225$ eggs per person per year, or about 19 dozen eggs per person per year.

3. The number from the American Egg Board is slightly higher than the number from the book; the American Egg Board claims that people eat more eggs than the book suggests.

4. *a.* Americans eat about 19 dozen eggs a year (from problem 2), so Americans eat about $1.5 \times 19 = 28.5$ pounds of eggs per year. According to the American Egg Board, Americans eat about 21 or 22 dozen eggs a year, weighing about 31.5 to 33 pounds.

b. Responses will vary. A toddler might weigh about this much, as would about three ten-pound bags of potatoes.

5. *a.* A typical egg carton that holds 1 dozen eggs measures about 11 inches long by 4 inches wide by 2.5 inches high. Its volume is about 110 cubic inches (11 x 4 x 2.5).

   b. 2090 cubic inches. (The length and width of the egg cartons don't change, but a stack of 19 egg cartons would be 47.5 inches tall.)

Solutions for "Did You Know?"

Answers will vary. See the three sample student responses on the CD-ROM.

Solutions for "Analyzing Data for Dr. Angus"

Students' responses will vary. Two solutions are described in the text. In addition, actual reponses from fourth-grade students appear on the CD-ROM, along with a discussion of each response.

References

Battista, Michael T. "The Development of a Cognition-Based Assessment System for Core Mathematics Concepts in Grades K–5." National Science Foundation project, 2001.

Chapin, Suzanne, Alice Koziol, Jennifer MacPherson, and Carol Rezba. *Navigating through Data Analysis and Probability in Grades 3–5. Priniciples and Standards for School Mathematics* Navigations Series. Reston, Va.: National Council of Teachers of Mathematics, 2003.

Curcio, Frances R., and Nadine S. Bezuk. *Understanding Rational Numbers and Proportions. Curriculum and Evaluation Standards for School Mathematics* Addenda Series, Grade 5–8, edited by Frances R. Curcio. Reston, Va.: National Council of Teachers of Mathematics, 1994.

Fennema, Elizabeth, Thomas P. Carpenter, Megan L. Franke, Linda Levi, Victoria R. Jacobs, and Susan B. Empson. "A Longitudinal Study of Learning to Use Children's Thinking in Mathematics Instruction." *Journal for Research in Mathematics Education* 27 (July 1996): 403–34.

Fraivillig, Judith. "Strategies for Advancing Children's Mathematical Thinking." *Teaching Children Mathematics* 7 (April 2001): 454–59.

Henningsen, Marjorie, and Mary K. Stein. "Mathematical Tasks and Student Cognition: Classroom-Based Factors That Support and Inhibit High-Level Mathematical Thinking and Reasoning." *Journal for Research in Mathematics Education* 28 (November 1997): 524–49.

Juraschek, Bill, and Amy Evans. "Ryan's Primes." *Teaching Children Mathematics* 3 (May 1997): 472–74.

National Council of Teachers of Mathematics (NCTM). *Principles and Standards for School Mathematics*. Reston, Va.: NCTM, 2000.

Passarello, Lisa M., and Francis Fennell. "Ideas: Every Beat of Your Heart." *Arithmetic Teacher* 39 (February 1992): 32–39.

Smith, Margaret Schwan, and Mary Kay Stein. "Selecting and Creating Mathematical Tasks: From Research to Practice." *Mathematics Teaching in the Middle School* 3 (February 1998): 344–50.

Stein, Mary Kay, Barbara W. Grover, and Marjorie Henningsen. "Building Student Capacity for Mathematical Thinking and Reasoning: An Analysis of Mathematical Tasks Used in Reform Classrooms." *American Educational Research Journal* 33 (October 1996): 455–88.

Stein, Mary Kay, and Margaret Schwan Smith. "Mathematical Tasks as a Framework for Reflection: From Research to Practice." *Mathematics Teaching in the Middle School* 3 (January 1998): 268–75.

Thompson, Denisse R., Michael T. Battista, Sally Mayberry, Karol L. Yeatts, and Judith S. Zawojewski. *Navigating through Problem Solving and Reasoning in Grade 5. Principles and Standards for School Mathematics* Navigations Series. Reston, Va.: National Council of Teachers of Mathematics, forthcoming (a).

———. *Navigating through Problem Solving and Reasoning in Grade 6. Principles and Standards for School Mathematics* Navigations Series. Reston, Va.: National Council of Teachers of Mathematics, forthcoming (b).

Tierney, Cornelia, Mark Ogonowski, Andee Rubin, and Susan J. Russell. *Different Shapes, Equal Pieces*. Menlo Park, Calif.: Dale Seymour Publications, 1998.

Yeatts, Karol L., Michael T. Battista, Sally Mayberry, Denisse R. Thompson, and Judith S. Zawojewski. *Navigating through Problem Solving and Reasoning in Grade 3. Principles and Standards for School Mathematics* Navigations Series. Reston, Va.: National Council of Teachers of Mathematics, 2004.

Yolles, Arlene. "Making Connections with Prime Numbers." *Mathematics Teaching in the Middle School* 7 (October 2001): 84–86.

Suggested Reading

Hatfield, Mary, Nancy Edwards, Gary Bitter, and Jean Morrow. *Mathematics Methods for Elementary and Middle School Teachers*. New York: John Wiley and Sons, 2000.

Mayberry, Sally C., and John B. Bath. *Student Resource Manual to Accompany Mathematics for Elementary Teachers: An Interactive Approach*. Philadelphia: Harcourt Brace, 1993.

Seymour, Dale. *Favorite Problems*. Palo Alto, Calif.: Seymour Publications, 1982.

Smith, Margaret Schwan. "Redefining Success in Mathematics Teaching and Learning." *Mathematics Teaching in the Middle School* 5 (February 2000): 378–86.

Wood, Terry, and Turner-Vorbeck, Tammy. "Extending the Conception of Mathematics Teaching." *Beyond Classical Pedagogy: Teaching Elementary School Mathematics*. Mahweh, N.J.: Erlbaum, 2001.

Zawojewski, Judith S. "Polishing a Data Task: Seeking Better Assessment." *Teaching Children Mathematics* 2 (February 1996): 372–78.

Zawojewski, Judith S., Richard Lesh, and Lyn English. "A Models and Modeling Perspective on the Role of Small Group Learning Activities." In *Beyond Constructivism*: *A Models and Modeling Perspective on Problem Solving, Learning, and Instruction in Mathematics and Science Education*, edited by Helen Doerr and Richard Lesh, pp. 337–58. Mahwah, N.J.: Erlbaum, 2003.

Children's Literature

Teachers may wish to incorporate appropriate literature into the investigations in this book. For children's books that are appropriate for particular mathematics topics, teachers may refer to *The Wonderful World of Mathematics: A Critically Annotated List of Children's Books in Mathematics*, by Diane Thiessen, Margaret Matthias, and Jacqueline Smith (Reston, Va.: NCTM, 1989). The examples of children's literature that are cited in the text follow:

Ash, Russell. *Incredible Comparisons*. London: Dorling Kindersley, 1996.

Jenkins, Steve. *Biggest, Strongest, Fastest*. New York: Tichnor and Fields, 1995.

Lasky, Kathryn. *The Librarian Who Measured the Earth*. Boston: Little, Brown and Company, 1994.

Morgan, Rowland. *In the Next Three Seconds…*. New York: Lodestar Books, 1997.

Wells, Robert E. *Is a Blue Whale the Biggest Thing There Is?* Morton Grove, Ill.: Albert Whitman and Company, 1993.

———. *What's Faster than a Speeding Cheetah?* Morton Grove, Ill.: Albert Whitman and Company, 1997.

———. *What's Smaller than a Pygmy Shrew?* Morton Grove, Ill.: Albert Whitman and Company, 1995.

Teachers may also wish to refer to the following books:

- *Exploring Mathematics through Literature: Articles and Lessons for Prekindergarten through Grade 8*, edited by Diane Thiessen (NCTM 2004). This book provides classroom examples of the use of children's literature to teach problem solving, representation, and reasoning.

- *New Visions for Linking Literature and Mathematics*, by David J. Whitin and Phyllis Whitin (NCTM/National Council of Teachers of English 2004). This book helps teachers find and use age-appropriate children's books with mathematical content.